JUDIASM
IN STONE

*The Archaeology
of Ancient Synagogues*

JUDAISM IN STONE

THE ARCHAEOLOGY OF ANCIENT SYNAGOGUES

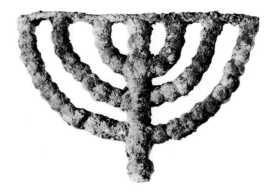

HERSHEL SHANKS

Preface by Yigael Yadin

HARPER & ROW, PUBLISHERS
New York , Hagerstown, San Francisco, London

BIBLICAL ARCHAEOLOGY SOCIETY
Washington, D.C.

To the memory of
E. L. SUKENIK (1889-1953)
and
MICHAEL AVI-YONAH (1904-1974)
Distinguished scholars, lovers of Zion,
and pioneers in ancient synagogue
archaeology

Co-published by:

The Biblical Archaeology Society   and   Harper & Row, Publishers, Inc.
1737 H Street, N.W.   10 E. 53 Street
Washington, D.C. 20006   New York, N.Y. 10022

Published simultaneously in Canada by Fitzhenry &
Whiteside Limited, Toronto.

Published simultaneously in Israel by Steimatzky's Agency Limited,
Tel Aviv.
First Edition

Design by Judith Mays

Printed in the United States of America

ISBN: 0-06-0672188

Library of Congress Cataloging in Publication Data
Shanks, Hershel.
  Judaism in stone.
  Includes index.
  1. Synagogues. 2. Jews—Antiquities. I. Title.
  DS111.7.S47 956.95'2 78-11722

CONTENTS

ACKNOWLEDGEMENTS

In this book I have tried to open a little known—but exciting—range of scholarship to the general reader. I could not have done this without the help of those dedicated and generous scholars who have devoted much of their lives to the subject, and to them I am deeply grateful:

To Michael Avi-Yonah, who, at the time of his untimely death, was professor of archaeology and of the history of art at The Hebrew University of Jerusalem and one of the world's pre-eminent authorities on the period of Jewish history covered by this book. It was he who should have written this book. He reviewed my entire manuscript as it existed shortly before his death and made many helpful suggestions and corrections.

To E. E. Urbach, professor of Talmud at The Hebrew University and a world leader in the critical study of the Talmud, who helped me to locate myself in the complex world of Chapters 10 and 11.

To Lee I. Levine, a brillant young American scholar, now a lecturer at The Hebrew University, who combines a rare mastery of the world of rabbinics and the world of archaeology. From his vantage point, he was able to give me a number of valuable insights for which I am deeply grateful.

To Gideon Foerster, of the Israel Department of Antiquities, whose contributions to synagogue archaeology have already made him a leader of a new generation of synagogue archaeologists.

To Eric M. Meyers, Professor of Jewish Studies at Duke University, excavator of the ancient synagogue at Shema and the ancient synagogue at Meiron, and America's leading authority on synagogue archaeology, whose scholarship saved me from a number of blunders.

To Dan Bahat of the Israel Department of Antiquities and the excavator of the ancient synagogue at Beth Shean, who continues to amaze me with his knowledge. His contributions to this book are many and detailed.

To Dan Barag of The Hebrew University, former editor of the *Israel Exploration Journal*, and excavator of the ancient synagogue at Ein Gedi.

More than anyone else he taught me what an actual dig of an ancient synagogue is.

Each of these scholars read all or part of my manuscript and made valuable suggestions, both large and small. Their collective contribution to this book has been enormous. However, final judgment on debatable matters has been mine alone, and the kindness of these scholars in reviewing my work should not be read as agreement with my judgments. The responsibility for the inevitable remaining errors is also mine.

Charles Fenyvesi, editor of the *National Jewish Monthly*, deftly edited the text. Jenifer Gruber edited and proofread the text and made every effort to keep me consistent in spelling and capitalization. Debra Allison carefully checked the footnotes and prepared the index. My secretaries Kathleen Hnat and Linda Holman provided the same invaluable assistance on this as on other projects. My thanks to them all.

I am deeply grateful to my family for their encouragement, interest, and support—my wife Judy and my daughters Elizabeth and Julia.

Hershel Shanks

PREFACE

Perhaps I may be forgiven if I confess how many happy personal memories this engaging book evokes in me. I was, if not suckled, at least raised as a youth on the subject of ancient synagogues. During the years I was growing up, ancient synagogues were almost a preoccupation of my father E. L. Sukenik—and therefore of mine. I remember his travelling about by horseback—through the Galilee, the Golan, and even northern Jordan—studying the ancient synagogues that had already been identified and searching for the remains of those which had not yet been discovered.

In the mid-1920's, when he received a stipend from Cyrus Adler to study at Dropsie College in Philadelphia, there was no question about his dissertation topic: ancient synagogues, of course. When he returned to Palestine after receiving his Ph.D., he continued to pursue his interest in the subject. He excavated Beth Alpha, Hamath Tiberias, as well as other synagogues, and widely published the results of his excavations—and horseback rides—in both the local press and scholarly journals.

Then in 1931, he was invited to deliver the Schweich Lectures before the British Academy. The subject: "Ancient Synagogues in Palestine and Greece". These lectures were later published in book form. Except for collections of articles, that book was the last to be published which canvasses the subject as a whole—until now. Not surprisingly, the materials which archaeologists have discovered since 1931 are enormous.

Judaism in Stone by Hershel Shanks brings the subject up to date. It is a fascinating description and interpretation of these ancient synagogue remains, some of which pre-date the Roman destruction of the Temple.

Unfortunately, most scholars do not know how to tell their stories in language the layman can understand. On the other hand, most popular writers are unable accurately to penetrate the scholar's technical apparatus and the specialist's jargon. Happily, Hershel Shanks has a flair for combining the understanding of a scholar with the felicity of language of a professional writer. In all his writings, but especially in this book on ancient synagogues, he has demonstrated an ability to translate scholarly archaeological materials into a popular genre without sacrificing either accuracy or breadth of understanding.

Strangely enough, the period of Jewish history with which this book deals is often neglected, especially by the general public. Touching these stones, so to speak, will give most readers a new understanding of a central Jewish institution (the synagogue), an introduction to a formative period of Jewish history (the Talmudic period), as well as an explanation of how archaeology provides new evidence for understanding the past. The reader will also frankly face a number of unsolved problems.

As an up-to-date introduction to ancient synagogues, I know of nothing I could recommend more than Hershel Shanks' book *Judaism in Stone*.

Yigael Yadin

Jerusalem

1 ✡ THE STORY OF ANCIENT SYNAGOGUES

Its strands are history, archaeology, a revolutionary concept, and controversial findings

This bronze head of the Emperor Hadrian was recently found on an Israeli kibbutz. Hadrian crushed the Second Jewish Revolt (132-135 C.E.) and built a Roman city named Aelia Capitolina on the site of Jewish Jerusalem.

The story of ancient synagogues is threefold. First, it is a stirring archaeological saga. Second, it recounts the development of Judaism's central religious institution. Third, it provides unsuspected insights into an epoch of Jewish history.

Nearly 200 ancient synagogues dot the Mediterranean littoral—from ancient Babylonia west to Italy and Tunisia, perhaps even to Spain. They date from the days when the Temple still stood in Jerusalem to the Arab conquest of the seventh century.

Major events of Jewish history occurred during this period. The first Jewish revolt against imperial Rome ended in 70 C.E. with the destruction of Jerusalem and the Temple. Sixty years later, the second Jewish revolt against Rome, intellectually sparked by Rabbi Akiba but politically and militarily led by Bar-Kochba, also culminated in death and destruction. This time Jews were banned from Jerusalem, which the Emperor Hadrian rebuilt as a Roman city he named Aelia Capitolina; the ensuing Hadrianic persecutions placed as heavy a yoke on the survivors of this abortive struggle for freedom as the Jews had yet known. But ultimately, the resulting emergence of rabbinic Judaism was significantly more important than the tragedies themselves. In the three to four hundred years that followed Rome's military victories, the *Midrash*, that unparalleled storehouse of homiletic elaboration of Scripture, took life; the *Mishnah*, the first and thereafter central collection of post-Scriptural Jewish law, was compiled; and around this core, that towering monument of rabbinic Judaism, the Talmud, was created.

The ancient synagogues we examine in this book form part of the history of a 700-year period. But they play an especially important role in understanding post-destruction Judaism. For the period *before* the destruction of the Second Temple, the historian has available a very considerable body of contemporary, or nearly contemporary, literary evidence from which to

11

reconstruct history—the late books of the Bible, the Apocrypha and pseud-epigrapha, Philo, Josephus, the New Testament, and, now, the Dead Sea Scrolls. But, for the centuries that follow, we have little beyond rabbinic literature. Because of the paucity of contemporary post-destruction literature reflecting more than one viewpoint, the evidence of ancient synagogues often provides a principal historical source for understanding Judaism during the post-destruction period.

These ancient synagogues provide more than a background to history for they also tell a story of their own—the story of the development of Judaism's central religious institution. During this period, the synagogue emerged and developed its unique character which has in many respects endured till the present.

Our story begins before the Roman destruction of Jerusalem when the central religious institution of Judaism was the Temple. Its focal ritual was animal sacrifice. Into its sacred precincts only the priests were allowed. To its Holy of Holies only the high priest himself could enter, and even then only once in the annual cycle, on the holiest day of the year, *Yom Kippur*. What occurred in the Temple could not be repeated elsewhere for the Temple was in some mystical, ineffable way the home of God Himself, the Lord's dwelling place. To build another Temple elsewhere could only be a rejection of a centralized religious authority.

The synagogue which ~~ultimately~~ replaced the destroyed Temple was totally different in each of these respects. The synagogue was not a place for professional priests; it was a place for the people. Its Hebrew name, *beit knesset*, as well as the Greek word synagogue, means house of assembly, a place where the people gather. Its focal ritual was not sacrifice, but the public reading of the Law and prayer. In the synagogue the worshipper sought communication with God, unmediated by any priest.* Even those who led the communal prayers were laymen. Instead of a single centralized institution, a synagogue could be established wherever a quorum of ten Jews felt the need to have one. The destruction of a synagogue—by no means an infrequent occurrence—was the destruction of a building only, not of a congregation. The survivors could, and did, assemble anywhere, in public or in private, and perform the same synagogue ritual with the same effectiveness as they had always done.

It is difficult for us to realize today what a thoroughly novel concept the idea of a synagogue was.[1] An eminent Jewish scholar has called its creation "a great revolutionary act of Judaism," "a spiritualization of divine worship."[2] Grounded in collective worship by the community, in which every Jew participated, the synagogue, in the words of a modern Christian scholar, "was a radical departure from anything the world had yet seen."[3]

The nineteenth century savant Ernest Renan called the synagogue "the most original and most fecund creation of the Jewish people." Both the church and the mosque are generally recognized as the spiritual daughters of the synagogue.[4]

The great Harvard scholar George Foot Moore summarized the role and influence of the synagogue this way:

[Judaism's] persistent character, and, it is not too much to say, the very preservation of its fortunes, it owes more than anything else to the synagogue. Nor is it

---

*The rabbi was an expert in the Law and a teacher. He was not and is not a mediator between man and God. In this period, he did not even lead the people in communal prayer.

Caesarea—This inscription was found in the synagogue at Caesarea. Written in Greek, it reads as follows: "Beryllos the *archisynagogus* and administrator, the son of Justus, made the mosaic work of the *triclinium* at his own expense." This is a typical donor's inscription, except for the mention of the *triclinium* or Roman style dining room.

for Judaism alone that it had this importance. It determined the type of Christian worship, which in the Greek and Roman world of the day might otherwise have taken the form of a mere mystery; and, in part directly, in part through the church, it furnished the model to Mohammed. Thus Judaism gave to the world not only the fundamental ideas of these great monotheistic religions but the institutional form in which they have perpetuated and propagated themselves.[5]

Part of the reason for the success of the synagogue in holding the Jewish people together was that it was so much more than just a house of prayer where the Law was publicly read. Equally important, it was a house of study—even of scholarship. It was also a community center, a meeting house, a hostel, a place where the people celebrated together, and a place where they wept together at the burial of their dead. One synagogue inscription records the gift of a mosaic floor in the synagogue's *triclinium*, a Roman style dining area. The synagogue dispensed charity and often served as a depository of funds and of communal treasures. Coin hoards are a common find in synagogue excavations. At Caesarea, for example, a community chest containing more than 3700 Byzantine coins was uncovered in the synagogue. Court proceedings were another synagogue activity and here punishments were meted out.[6]

As the eminent Jewish historian Salo Baron has observed, "The synagogue building was used for all imaginable communal purposes . . . In the synagogue, the community had a living center for all its public life".[7]

It is common to think of ancient Jewish life during this period as serene, pietistic and of one mold. In this vein, one might suppose that to see one ancient synagogue is to see them all. But nothing could be further from the truth. The image of Jewish life reflected in synagogue remains is rich, vibrant, and varied. Time and time again, we shall see the scholars stubbing their erudite toes in their efforts to bring some kind of order into all this variety.

Rather than serene uniformity, we find in these ancient synagogues much of the tensions and dissensions, the piety and the secularism that reminds us of our own time. We shall see poor, small Jewish communities, and large rich ones; sophisticated urban communities and rural folk communities; communities that appear to have followed the letter of the Law

13

and communities that interpreted the Law more flexibly. But above all, we get a picture of Jews striving to create a Judaism meaningful to them, and arriving at a wide variety of answers, each uniquely true to the ancestral message.

The discovery and excavation of these ancient synagogues is itself a stirring story. Perhaps the reader will be able to recapture the excitement of those excavators who were unearthing synagogues forty and fifty years ago when only a few were known, when these archaeological pioneers

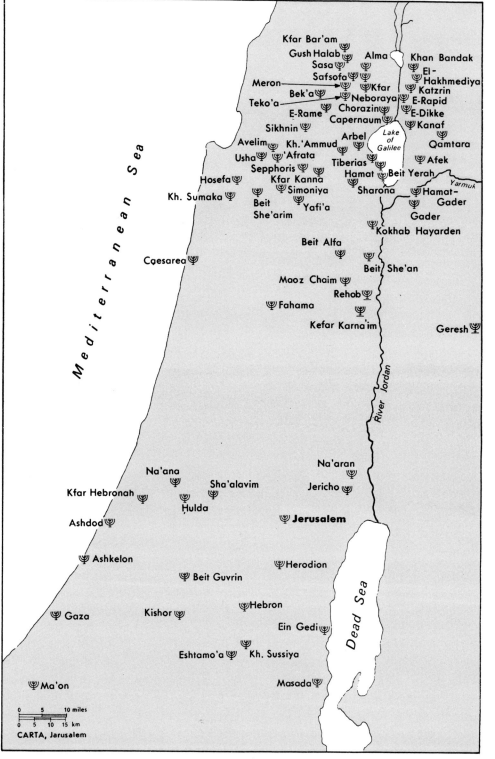

The map indicates some of the sites in Israel and adjacent areas where ancient synagogue remains have been found.

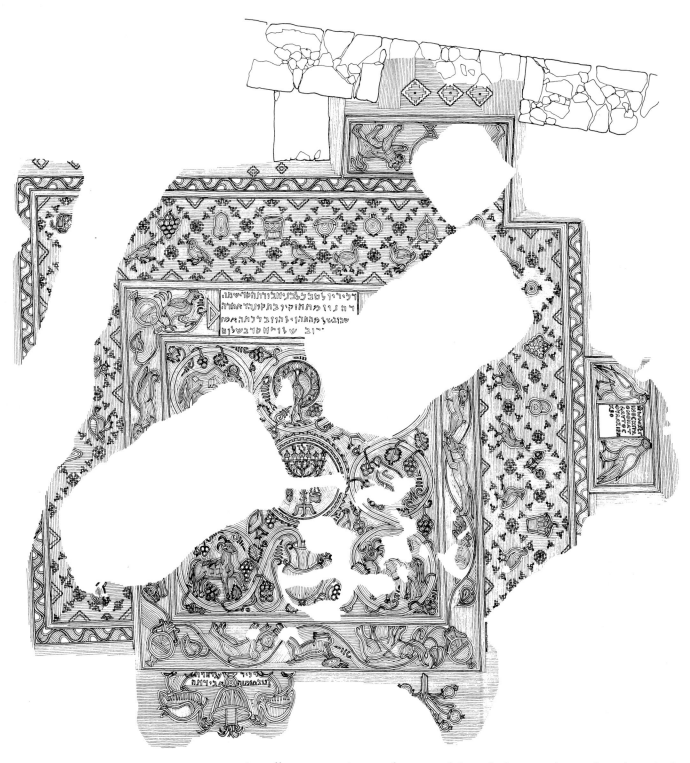

were virtually uncovering a chapter of Jewish history heretofore based almost solely on literary sources.

We can perhaps imagine the surprise of the archaeologists at finding a synagogue dating from the time the Talmud was created or another that reached back to the time when the Temple still stood in Jerusalem, of synagogues with mosaic floors or biblical wall paintings, of *menorot* that lit Jewish prayers 1500 years ago and a *bema* upon which the leaders of the Sanhedrin might have stood.

We might also imagine a different series of surprises, a series of exclamations that reflect the scholars' shock at evidence that the Judaism of this

15

period was not just a monolithic pietism. To the surprise of finding a synagogue decorated with biblical pictures in what may have seemed an infraction of the Second Commandment's prohibition against images, there was added the shock of finding an eagle reminiscent of the symbol of imperial Rome, cupids upholding Graeco-Roman wreaths, King David as Orpheus taming wild beasts, vintners treading grapes in a Bacchic scene, and even the signs of the zodiac encircling the Greek sun-god Helios in his chariot flying through the heavens and putting the night to flight. What in the world was all this doing in synagogue after synagogue? Scholars' attempts to answer such questions form another strand of the story.

The story of ancient synagogues cannot yet be completed. New finds are continually adding chapters and requiring changes in old interpretations. Some of this account may be outdated by the time it reaches the printed page. But this only makes it more, not less, exciting, and we shall try to make this account as current as this morning's newspaper.

Hammath-Tiberias—A mosaic synagogue pavement containing a zodiac. A wall was later built over the zodiac, but we can still see in the center the Greek sun-god Helios with the rays of the sun emanating from his head. At the top of the mosaic is a Torah ark and a *menorah*.

16

2 ✡ SYNAGOGUES BEFORE THE ROMAN DESTRUCTION OF THE TEMPLE

Did synagogues exist when the Temple still stood in Jerusalem?

Readers of Yigael Yadin's memorable volume *Masada* can easily imagine the thrill of finding on this desolate mountain fortress a synagogue which pre-dated the Roman destruction of the Jerusalem Temple, perhaps by as much as 80 years.

Here is Professor Yadin relating his momentous discovery:

During the first season we already dared to suggest, albeit with considerable hesitation, that [the building we were excavating] was perhaps a synagogue.... If what we had just unearthed was indeed a synagogue, then this was a discovery of front rank importance in the field of Jewish archaeology and certainly one of the most important finds in Masada. For up to then the very earliest synagogues discovered in Israel belonged to the end of the 2nd or beginning of the 3rd century A.D. There were no remains of any synagogue from the period of the Second Temple.[1]

What Professor Yadin says is accurate.[2] However, many readers unfamiliar with the history of synagogues erroneously assumed that Professor Yadin's find was the first and only evidence for the existence of a synagogue prior to the Roman destruction of the Temple.[3]

In fact, we have abundant proof that the synagogue was a flourishing and highly developed institution hundreds of years before the Roman destruction of the Temple. Professor Yadin's excavations at Masada marked the discovery of the first synagogue *building* remains which predated the Roman destruction.

This is not intended to detract from the importance of the Masada synagogue. It is invaluable to have a building that served as a synagogue before the Romans destroyed the Temple. But it is equally important to keep this discovery in perspective. We know a great deal about the synagogue as an institution before the destruction of the Temple in 70 C.E.

We even have archaeological evidence for a synagogue in Israel which pre-dates the Masada synagogue, although no trace has been found of the synagogue building itself. The dedication inscription alone survives. Moreover, the inscription belonged to a synagogue not in the wastes of the Judean wilderness such as Masada, but to a synagogue in the Holy City itself where the Temple was readily accessible.

This inscription was found in 1913 during excavations conducted by the French archaeologist Captain Raymond Weill in the oldest inhabited part of Jerusalem, known as the hill of Ophel or the City of David (the hill of Ophel is where King David's Jerusalem is located). The synagogue inscription was not discovered in its original setting; it had apparently been thrown into the cistern where it was found after the destruction of the city. Its contents are remarkable. Written in well-chiselled Greek on Jerusalem limestone, it reads as follows:

Theodotus, son of Vettenos, priest and archisynagogus, son of an archisynagogus and grandson of an archisynagogus, built this synagogue for the reading of the Law and for the teaching of the Commandments, and the hostel and the cham-

Masada—Herod built a palace and fortress on this diamond-shaped, flat-top mountain in the midst of the Judean wilderness. On the left side of the mountain is the so-called snake path—the approach to the fortress from the Dead Sea side. The squares to the right of the mountain—1300 feet below—are the remains of the Roman camps. Between the Roman camps and the top of the mountain is a ramp built by Roman soldiers to gain access to the fortress when it was defended by the Zealots.

bers and the waterfittings for the accommodation of those who, coming from abroad, have need of it, of which synagogue the foundations were laid by his fathers and by the Elders and by Simonides.

Scholars date the inscription to King Herod's reign (37 B.C.E.-4 B.C.E.). But by referring to the construction of the synagogue at least two generations earlier, the inscription points to the presence of a synagogue in Jerusalem as early as 150 years before the Roman destruction of the Temple.

This synagogue appears to be a highly developed institution. The inscriber tells us that it was the place where the Law was read and where the commandments of the Lord were taught. Thus already at that early stage, education was a primary function of the synagogue. That the synagogue met this responsibility was no doubt one reason it was permitted to exist in the Holy City, side by side with the Temple.

The synagogue was—and continued to be—much more than a place where the Law was publicly read and a school. Attached to it was a kind of hostel where travelers and strangers could spend the night and take their meals. (In our own day, a few sleeping rooms are often attached to private clubs, like country clubs, faculty clubs and eating clubs. Two thousand years ago—and thereafter for much of Jewish history—the synagogue, open to all Jews, functioned in this way; Jews had no need of hotels.) We can infer that the rooms in this Jerusalem synagogue were often used by pilgrims who came to the Holy City for one of the three great Temple festivals—*Pesach* (Passover), *Succot* (Tabernacles) and *Shavuot* (the Feast of Weeks)—or perhaps just to see the Temple before they died. The rooms must have been commodious, as we learn from the inscription, for they offered sleeping accommodations as well as plumbing facilities. One can guess that attached to the synagogue was a *mikveh* or ritual immersion bath for women, as well as a public bath for men. Communal activities of local membership no doubt took place in the synagogue, although major events of city-wide or national significance focussed on the Temple.

Despite the wide range of activities cited in the inscription, no mention is made of public prayer offered in the synagogue. The inscription tells us that the Law was read—supporting the thesis that public reading of the Law was the most important element in early synagogue ritual. Whether public communal prayers were recited at all in pre-destruction synagogues is an open question. Perhaps before the destruction of the Temple, it was thought that public prayer could be offered only in the Temple, regarded as God's own dwelling place. The omission from this important inscription of any mention of public prayer lends support to those who argue that institutionalized public prayer became part of synagogue ritual only after the destruction of the Temple.

The Jerusalem synagogue inscription also provides contemporaneous evidence for synagogue organization. The head of the synagogue was called *archisynagogus*. In Hebrew, the term was *rosh ha-knesset*, or head of the assembly, just as the synagogue itself was—and is—called *beit knesset* or house of assembly. The position of *archisynagogus* appears to have been hereditary. This continued to be the practice for some time, as we learn from inscriptions found in Rome which refer to various *archisynagogi* as the descendants of others who held this title. The duties of the *archisynagogus* were apparently much like those of today's synagogue president. And, like the modern president, the power of the ancient *archisynagogus* was not absolute. From the Jerusalem inscription we learn that the synagogue was governed by a group referred to as the "Elders"—analogous to a modern synagogue's Board of Directors. It was they who appear to have made the decision to construct this particular synagogue and therefore they had the honor of laying the foundation stone, together with a dignitary named Simonides—was he perhaps invited for the ceremony to address the congregation?—who was so well-known at the time that he needed no further identification.

Another curious thing about this inscription is that even though it belonged to a synagogue in the Holy City itself, it is written in Greek and uses Greek rather than Hebrew terms. Perhaps this synagogue was built for diaspora Jews whose mother tongue was Greek. Whether or not this was the case, the inscription reveals the extent to which the Greek language and culture permeated Judaism. Indeed, there are more synagogue inscriptions in Greek—even in Palestine—than in Hebrew or Aramaic.

A final puzzle about this inscription is that it refers to Theodotus as a priest as well as an *archisynagogus*—yet his father and grandfather are not identified as priests. We can only guess what the nature of his priesthood was or whether at this time a priest had a different function than the *kohanim* had in later days.

The Jerusalem synagogue inscription—or Theodotus inscription, as it is known to archaeologists—is one of the most dramatic archaeological finds of the century. Like the Masada synagogue, it serves to confirm rather than to challenge our expectations regarding the existence of pre-destruction synagogues. For the Talmud tells us that before the Roman destruction of the Temple, there were 394 synagogues in Jerusalem[4] and gives us much the same picture of the synagogue as the one offered by the Jerusalem synagogue inscription.

At the turn of the twentieth century, it was the fashion among scholars to consider the talmudic assertion that there were 394 synagogues in Jerusalem at the time of the Roman destruction as "the usual *aggadic* exaggeration". However, today, many scholars believe that this figure might well be accurate. Modern Jerusalem has considerably more synagogues than this. In modern Israel, there are more than 6,000 synagogues.[5] Most of these synagogues are quite small—as were most of the ancient synagogues. And while the population of Jerusalem at the time of the Roman destruction of the Temple has been estimated at more than 100,000[6] compared to a post-1967 Jewish population of three times this figure, religion *per se* held a far more central place in the lives of the people then than now. So the talmudic figure is not necessarily an exaggeration.*

Nor is there any reason to suspect a conflict between the Temple and the synagogue. The Talmud tells us of a synagogue that was located on the Temple Mount itself, but mentions no objection to it.[8] With all its reverence for the Temple, the Talmud would surely have recorded a conflict between the two institutions.

The Talmud is not the only ancient literary source to attest to the widespread existence of synagogues both in Palestine and in the diaspora before 70 C.E. The New Testament, the Hellenistic Jewish philosopher Philo, the Jewish historian Josephus and the third Book of Maccabees[9] are all in agreement that the synagogue was a well-established institution long before the Roman destruction of Jerusalem.

How far back in time, then, did the synagogue exist? From Egypt we have evidence of a synagogue as early as the third century B.C.E. In 1902, a synagogue dedication inscription carved in marble was uncovered 12 miles southeast of Alexandria in the little village of Schedia. Early synagogues in Egypt were built under the patronage of the ruler, and it was therefore customary to dedicate the building to him. That is the substance of the Schedia inscription from Egypt which reads in Greek:

In honor of King Ptolemy and of Queen Berenice, his sister and wife, and of their children, the Jews have dedicated this synagogue.[10]

This simple inscription speaks volumes about the Jewish community of the time and its relationship to the larger gentile community.[11]

Most scholars believe that the origins of the synagogue are to be found long before the time of the Schedia inscription, and not in Egypt, but in Babylonia during the exile following the destruction of the First Temple in 586 B.C. It was in response to the destruction of their Temple that the Jewish people created this remarkable institution—but in response to the *first* destruction, not the *second* destruction. Bereft of their central shrine, deported to a strange land, their communal institutions destroyed, the Jewish people created the synagogue from the ashes—a new institution, unknown to the pagan world, that was to bind them together, educate their children, teach them their laws, and enable them as a community to continue to relate to their universal God.

With considerable persuasiveness other scholars have gone even further, and have attempted to trace the source of the synagogue to the First Temple days in Palestine itself. According to them, incipient synagogues may be found in the early prayer meetings which can be inferred from a number of passages in the Hebrew Bible.[12] Particularly intriguing is a passage from Psalm 74 which speaks of God's adversaries having burnt up all the "meeting places of God" (*moadai el*) in the land. The best modern authority now holds that this psalm was written shortly after the Babylonian destruction[13] and refers to the havoc wreaked by the Babylonians while the First Temple still stood. What were these meeting places of God which the psalmist speaks of in First Temple days, as if his audience would

*In ancient times Jewish communities of any substantial size had more than one synagogue. Tiberias, on the Sea of Galilee, for example, had 13 synagogues at the end of third century, C.E.; Sepphoris had 18.[7]

be familiar with them? Were they synagogues or forerunners of synagogues?

Perhaps these meeting places of God originated during the reign of King Hezekiah (late 8th century) or possibly King Josiah (late 7th century). Both of these Judean kings instituted religious reforms. They attempted to centralize worship in Jerusalem and suppressed Hebrew as well as pagan cultic installations outside the Holy City. In I Kings 23:8 we learn that Josiah destroyed *bamot* (altars or so-called high places) from Geba to Beer-Sheba. Some scholars have suggested that the "meeting places of God" were originally designed to replace the prohibited *bamot* and in response to the spiritual vacuum created by the destruction of these local shrines.[14]

Whether the origin of the synagogue is to be found in the Holy Land or Babylonia, the synagogue at Masada—and a contemporaneous synagogue at Herodium—are the oldest synagogue *buildings* which archaeologists have yet uncovered.[15] And this is, as Professor Yadin has said, "a discovery of front rank importance in the field of Jewish archaeology".

Masada is the colossal mountain fortress constructed by King Herod (37 B.C.E.-4 B.C.E.) on the shores of the Dead Sea in the midst of the

Masada—An aerial view of the synagogue which was built into the casemate wall enclosing the mountain fortress. (A casemate wall consists of two parallel walls divided by partitions.) Note the sheer drop outside the wall at the bottom and right side of the picture. The synagogue walls are lined with benches. Five column-bases are visible inside the synagogue. Fragments of biblical books were found in the room in the corner of the synagogue, which may have served as the synagogue's *genizah*. The entrance to the synagogue is at the top.

Judean wilderness. Built on a diamond-shaped plateau that rises precipitously 1300 feet above the sea below, it is one of the most impressive sights in the Holy Land. The visitor cannot help but marvel at the Israelites' ability to build a sumptuous palace on top of an inaccessible mountain.

When the Jews revolted against Rome in 66 C.E., a small group of Jewish Zealots occupied Masada, and were joined by others who fled there after the fall of Jerusalem to the Romans in 70 C.E.[16] Secure in their mountain fortress, this tiny group of defiant Jews denied the power of imperial Rome and withstood seige for three years. Finally, in 73 C.E., when defeat was imminent, the survivors committed suicide rather than surrender to the Romans. Today, Israeli armored corps recruits are sworn in on Masada, pledging that "Masada shall not fall again"; a part of basic training in the Israeli army includes a trek and bivouac atop Masada. It is not uncommon to see one of these Israeli soldiers at sunrise saying his morning prayers in the world's oldest extant synagogue—a synagogue which is again functioning after 1900 years.

The Masada synagogue is located beside the northwestern wall of the fortress; in fact, the back wall of the synagogue is part of the fortress wall. The synagogue was built in two phases; the first phase is assigned to Herod and the second to the Zealots. The plan of the synagogue during the Herodian period is shown in the illustration. Through the eastern entrance, one came into a small room (39 feet by 48 feet), containing five pillars which created a central nave and aisles on two sides. In front of the synagogue was a small ante-room.

None of the decoration inside or outside the synagogue has survived; we can only speculate as to what it might have been. On the walls of Herod's palace and villa, frescoes were painted in imitation of stone and marble—a similar treatment might have been given to the synagogue walls. The synagogue floors probably consisted of flagstones since no trace of mosaics was found.

When the Zealots occupied Masada, they made a number of changes in the synagogue. First, they tore down the wall between the ante-room and the synagogue, thereby enlarging the synagogue room. Second, they lined the walls with four tiers of plastered benches. Third, they removed two of the old Herodian columns so they could build a small room in one corner of the synagogue. We do not know the purpose of this small room. It could be entered only from the synagogue room. Perhaps the Torah scrolls

First plan at right
Masada—A plan of the synagogue as built by Herod. An outer room served as an entrance hall. Inside the synagogue were columns.

Second plan at right
Masada—A plan of the synagogue as modified by the Zealots. Removing the wall which stood between the entrance hall and the synagogue in Herod's time, the Zealots replaced it with two columns to provide the roof support previously supplied by the wall. They also added the room in the corner of the synagogue. The walls of this room supported the roof, so two of the columns from Herod's synagogue (which were now inside the corner room) could be safely removed, thus allowing full utilization of the corner room.

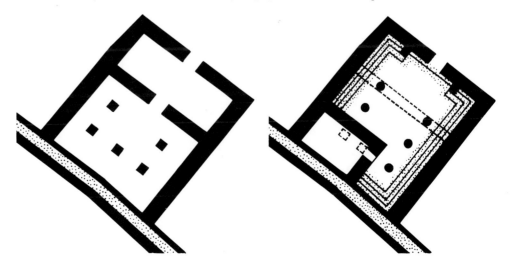

23

Masada—A closer view of the interior of the synagogue. Benches line the walls on left and right. The five columns have been partially reconstructed. The Israeli flag flies above the wall of the synagogue's corner room.

opposite
Masada—The walls of Herod's palace were painted to imitate marble, suggesting a similar style was used on the walls of the synagogue. Here a student volunteer is treating the surface to preserve it.

and possibly a wooden ark to house them were stored here.[17] This portable ark would then be brought into the synagogue for the service. As we shall see in later chapters, this was a common arrangement before a permanent structure for the Torah ark was built into the synagogue's prayer room.

Perhaps at this point we should ask a more basic question: How do we know this building was a synagogue? The most convincing evidence comes from two pits which the Zealots dug and which the archaeologists found in the little room the Zealots built in the corner of the synagogue. The pits were dug beneath the Zealot floor, but not so deep as to reach the Herodian floor under it. In each of the pits, remains of biblical scrolls were found—Deuteronomy in one and Ezekiel in the other.

This then was the Zealot *genizah*—the traditional burial ground for worn out holy writings the destruction of which is forbidden by religious law. (Old *genizah* caches provide scholars with some of their best finds. The most famous is the so-called Cairo *genizah*, recovered in Egypt by Sol-

omon Schechter in 1897. His documents are still being collated and published.)

There are other reasons to believe that this Masada building was a synagogue. The architecture is similar to that of some Galilean synagogues we shall look at later. An ostracon was found on the floor of the building inscribed "priestly tithe". The building was obviously some kind of public structure, and the benches installed by the Zealots indicate it was used for gatherings. Finally, the orientation of the building may support its identification as a synagogue but at the same time raises problems. The building is in one sense oriented toward Jerusalem. Someone who entered the building

Masada—A *mikveh* for ritual bathing. On the floor of the valley in the upper right are the remains of the square-shaped Roman camps.

from the east and faced the back of the building would be looking generally toward Jerusalem. As we shall see in later chapters, the problem is that before there was a permanent niche for the Torah ark, the *front* facade of the building customarily faced Jerusalem; in such synagogues the worshippers were supposed to enter the synagogue and then turn around to pray—and watch the portable ark being brought into the synagogue. If the worshippers at Masada had done this, they would be facing in the *opposite* direction from Jerusalem. Perhaps, as we have suggested, in the building's second phase the Torah was brought in during the service from the little room inside the synagogue, so the congregants did not have to turn around to see it being brought in. Perhaps there was a Torah shrine in the back wall facing Jerusalem, which has by now disappeared and which the worship-

Herodium—An artificial mountain built by Herod; on top, he constructed a fortress and palace, as well as a synagogue with an adjacent *mikveh* for ritual bathing.

pers faced without turning around upon entry. Another suggestion recently put forward by Gideon Foerster, a leading Israeli synagogue archaeologist, is that the building is perhaps not oriented toward Jerusalem at all.[18] It may be oriented toward the east, the general direction in which the doorway looks and the front facade faces. Pagan temples faced the rising sun and later Christian churches frequently followed this practice.

The Israelite Temple in Jerusalem too was oriented with its front facade to the east. A curious passage in the *Tosephta** tells us that the entrance facade of synagogues must face east, just as the Temple did.[19] Scholars have long puzzled over this passage which appears to contradict the *ha-*

Herodium—The synagogue in many details resembles the Masada synagogue, including the benches lining the walls. Four columns supported the roof. To the right of the synagogue entrance is the *mikveh.*

*Early rulings which were not incorporated into the Talmud.

lachic requirement that synagogues must be oriented toward Jerusalem. The *Tosephta* may preserve an earlier tradition in which synagogues faced east, rather than Jerusalem. Dr. Foerster suggests that this may be a tradition of the Second Temple period which, after the Temple's destruction, was gradually replaced by another tradition which required synagogues to be oriented not to the east, but toward the destroyed Temple. According to this theory, the orientation toward the site of the destroyed Temple ultimately became the norm and is preserved in the *Halacha*. Dr. Foerster's theory is certainly consistent with the fact that so many aspects of the post-destruction synagogue were designed to preserve the memory of the destroyed Temple.[20] And this theory would explain an eastern orientation of the Masada synagogue, as well as the orientation of several other synagogues.

Regardless of the orientation puzzle of the Masada synagogue, the totality of the evidence supports the building's identification as a synagogue, although far more convincingly with respect to the period when the Zealots occupied Masada than when Herod occupied it. But even during the Herodian period, the likelihood is that the building was a synagogue. Despite the fact that Herod was not one of the more religiously devout leaders of Israel, he made a mighty effort during his reign to win the favor of the traditional orthodox elements, and it is unlikely that he would have deprived those Jewish members of his entourage that accompanied him to Masada of a place to worship. (Among all the art found at Masada, there was not a single representation of a man or animal.) Then, in searching for a site for their synagogue, the Zealots chose a place which had already been a synagogue, in accordance with conservative tradition.

If the building at Masada was a synagogue, so was a similar structure dating from precisely the same period at Herodium.[21] Herodium, like Masada, was one of a series of fortress-palaces which Herod built on his eastern frontier. And Herodium, again like Masada, was magnificently situated atop a mountain with sheer drops, surrounded by desolation. Accord-

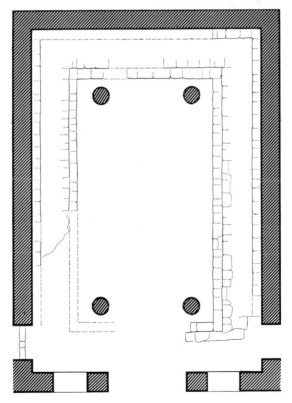

Herodium—A plan of the synagogue.

ing to Josephus, Herod was buried in Herodium, and the entire structure may have been built in the form of a giant mausoleum, with the crypt presumably underlying the large central tower at the east end of the round structure. (Unlike the other smaller towers, the larger tower appears to be solid down to its base, at which point it may have crypt chambers.) Herodium also contains a building remarkably similar to the Masada synagogue, including its orientation. Like the Masada synagogue, the Herodium synagogue had two phases; one when the fortress was occupied by Herod and the other when it was occupied by the Zealots who, as at Masada, added the tiers of benches along the walls.

Just outside the Herodium synagogue is a *mikveh*, or ritual immersion bath, which apparently served the Zealot community. Like two similar *mikvaot* found at Masada (which, however, were not adjacent to the synagogue), the Herodium *mikveh* meets all the traditional *halachic* requirements. It provides dramatic evidence that the Zealots who made their last stand against the Roman legions in the Judean wilderness were traditional orthodox Jews.

These archaeological fragments offer hints; a more complete picture of the synagogue before the Roman destruction of the Temple may be fleshed out by future discoveries. (See, for example, Chapter 9, which describes a recent excavation at a site where a pre-destruction synagogue may still be buried). What little we have uncovered reflects a well-established, complex, multifunctional institution which, while distinctly Jewish, absorbed much from the surrounding cultures—both in Palestine and in the diaspora.

opposite
Masada—Herod's palace on the northern end of the fortress. Built into the northwestern casemate wall surrounding the fortress was a synagogue—constructed by Herod and later remodelled by the Zealots who occupied Masada during the First Jewish Revolt against Rome (66 C.E.-70 C.E.). The Zealots on Masada held out until 73 C.E., when they committed suicide rather than surrender.

3 ✡ DISCOVERING ANCIENT SYNAGOGUES

By amateurs and professionals, through war and peace, under churches and mosques

A catalogue with the ponderous title, *The Second Revised Edition of the Ancient Synagogues of the Holy Land*,[1] was published in Jerusalem in 1972. It lists 134 sites where remains of ancient synagogues have been found. While the author's definition of the Holy Land is loose—it extends far beyond Israel's present ceasefire lines (to include Jordan, Syria, Lebanon and even Iraq)—this is still a surprisingly large list of ancient synagogues. Yet this compilation is already outdated. For new synagogue sites and remains of synagogues are being discovered in the Holy Land almost daily. The first revised edition of this catalogue was published in 1969; and by 1972, it was necessary to revise it again. Another revision is now needed.

Ancient synagogue remains are not confined to the Holy Land. They are liberally sprinkled over the map of the ancient diaspora in Egypt, Turkey, Yugoslavia, Italy, North Africa, and possibly even Spain. Here, too, new sites are being discovered. One of the most spectacular finds is at Sardis, the ancient capital of Lydia (now in Turkey) where archaeologists have uncovered the largest synagogue ever discovered—over 300 feet long, longer than a football field! The Talmud tells of a synagogue in Alexandria which was so large that the *hazzan* had to raise a scarf as a signal to the worshippers in the back who could not hear him, so they would know when to say "Amen."[2] This story was often rejected as a gross exaggeration until the discovery in Sardis.

We shall return to the Sardis synagogue; it is mentioned here only to warn that categorizing ancient synagoguges is hazardous: A new synagogue may be discovered tomorrow which contradicts today's generalizations. We shall nevertheless attempt to draw broad conclusions on the basis of the latest information, but the reader must accept these generalizations with caution, for what we do not know far exceeds what we know.

While the number of sites where synagogue remains have been found extends to the hundreds, this does not mean that in every case a substantial

opposite
Belvoir—This beautiful Crusader fortress overlooks the Jordan Valley. It was built in part with stones from an ancient synagogue.

part of the synagogue building is extant. In many cases, all that survives is a lintel, the capital of a pillar or an inscription. Often we cannot locate the synagogue site itself. The number of actual synagogue buildings with substantial parts standing is less than one hundred.

Until the late nineteenth century almost as many synagogues disappeared as were discovered. Synagogue ruins described by early pilgrims and even by explorers of recent centuries have disappeared without a trace. Had not the Franciscan monks purchased the famous Capernaum synagogue from its Arab owners in 1894 (the monks' interest in the synagogue derived from their belief that Jesus had preached there, rather than from its intrinsic archaeological value), even less would be left of this beautiful structure than what we have now. To protect the scarce white limestone of the Capernaum synagogue from further depradation, the Franciscans buried some of the structure. Other sites were not so fortunate, and the stones of these synagogues were carried off piece by piece for use in other buildings.

For this and other reasons, synagogue remains are found in the most unlikely places. The Jerusalem synagogue inscription discussed in a previous chapter was found in an ancient cistern. How it got there, who threw it there, and after what vicissitudes, we have no idea. At Yafa, or Yafia (a small Arab village near Nazareth, not to be confused with Jaffa near Tel-Aviv), a delicately carved lintel that once graced an entrance to a synagogue was found serving as a lintel in the window of a Greek Catholic Church. A *menorah* or seven-branched candelabra, flanked by two rosettes, is still visible on the church lintel.[3]

High above the heads of the worshippers in the Great Mosque of Gaza (Djami el-Kebir) on one of its lofty columns, a *menorah* has been carved. On its right is a *shofar* or ram's horn; on its left, a *lulav* (palm branch) and *etrog* (citron), used by Jews for the ancient festival of *Succot*. Below the *menorah* is an inscription in Hebrew ("Hannaniah, son of Jacob") and another in Greek. This column—and, we may assume, others of similar stone

35

which have no carving—helped to support the roof of a synagogue 1700 years ago, but nothing remains today except these columns, which are now part of the mosque.[4]

A crusader castle is an unlikely place to look for the remains of a synagogue. But in the world of ancient synagogues, the unlikely has become commonplace. In the 12th century C.E., on a height which affords a pano-

Gaza—A drawing of a columnar section of the Great Mosque of Gaza, showing, in the upper column, the location of a *menorah* and a Hebrew inscription.

Gaza—Details of columnar bas-relief. Enclosed in a hellenistic wreath is a three-footed *menorah* carved on a column originally part of a synagogue, now part of the structure of the Great Mosque of Gaza. The *lulav* and *etrog* on the left of the *menorah* and the *shofar* on the right are stylized, but recognizable. The inscription beneath is in Hebrew and Greek.

ramic view of the Jordan Valley far below, south of the Sea of Galilee, the venerable Order of St. John (the famous Hospitallers) constructed a magnificent fortress aptly named Belvoir, which defended a major Palestinian pass from the Moslems to the east. A historian of the period has called Belvoir "one of the greatest crusader achievements."[5] There, in 1967, a number of stones forming part of the crusader wall were found to have once been part of an ancient synagogue. Thus do the synagogues of antiquity survive.

The discovery of ancient synagogues is not confined to professional archaeologists. One ancient synagogue was found as a result of war. In September 1918, General Allenby's British forces, attempting to liberate Palestine from the Turks, met up with an Austrian-Turkish artillery unit at a point a few miles northwest of ancient Jericho. An Austrian shell missed its target and dug several feet beneath the surface into a hillock at Ein Duk. The shell uncovered the first mosaic floor of an ancient synagogue ever to be discovered. This is the famous synagogue of Na'aran, to which we shall return.

Another antique synagogue was found near Jericho by an Arab farmer

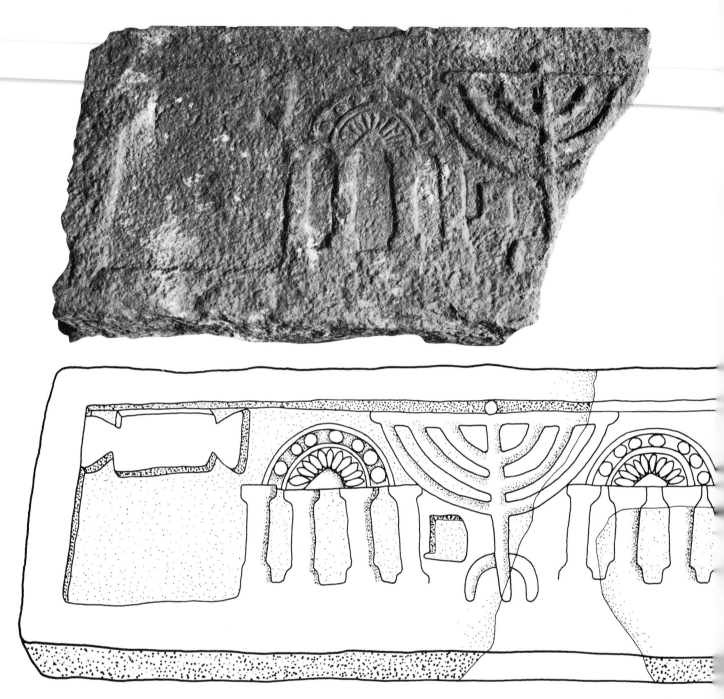

as he was digging trenches to plant banana trees. In one of the trenches he found the remains of an ancient synagogue with a beautiful mosaic floor well preserved—almost as if it had been freshly laid. When the Arab who owned the land decided to build a house over the mosaic, E.L. Sukenik, a pioneer in the field of ancient synagogue archaeology, attempted to raise enough money to buy the synagogue. Failing in this, Sukenik extracted a promise from the man to preserve the mosaic as part of his basement. All this took place in the years before the end of the British Mandate over Palestine. After Israel's rebirth in 1948, the mosaic floor near Jericho became part of Jordan, so few Jews—and no Israelis—were able to see it. When the area again became accessible to Israel in 1967 after the Six Day War, it was found that the Arab had been true to the promise he had made to Sukenik: The mosaic remained in perfect condition as the floor of his basement.[6] In the center of the mosaic is a lovely *menorah*, and, below it, a

above
Belvoir—A reconstruction of a lintel from an ancient synagogue, based on the two pieces found in secondary use in the fortress of Belvoir. The two extant pieces are at the top of this page and at the bottom of the opposite page. The two pieces are identified in the reconstruction by the shaded areas inside a line.

right
Belvoir—Archaeologist Ben-Dov's
reconstruction of the synagogue
entrance.

opposite and below
Belvoir—The piece of the lintel opposite contains a three-footed *menorah*
with a columned ark. In the upper
corner is a raised panel which looks as
if it was prepared for an inscription
that was never added. In the lower
right is an Aramaic inscription which,
according to archaeologist Ben-Dov
reads: " . . . who established this lintel
of their own and public funds. Amen.
Amen. Selah." Ben-Dov dates the
synagogue to the 3rd-4th century C.E.

Hebrew inscription from Psalm 125: "Peace unto Israel". On the right is a *shofar;* and on the left a *lulav*. Above the *menorah* is a Torah ark. As we shall see, these Jewish symbols are repeatedly found as decorations in ancient synagogues. A good capitalist, the owner of the house now charges visitors a small entrance fee to visit his basement, and he is well on his way to early retirement.

The beautiful mosaic at Beth Alpha in the Jezreel Valley was found in the same way as the Jericho synagogue, except that the farmers were Jewish, not Arab. Some early Jewish settlers who were reclaiming their barren land uncovered the Beth Alpha synagogue while digging an irrigation channel. It was like finding an ancient title deed to the land they were again making theirs. Today this beautiful synagogue is maintained by the National Parks Authority and is a major tourist stop. We shall look at it more closely later.

The accidental discovery of ancient synagogues continues. In the course of construction of the expressway to Rome's new international airport, Leonardo da Vinci, at Fiumicino, workmen in the 1960's discovered the unique synagogue of ancient Ostia, the only ancient synagogue building extant in Italy. A few years earlier, a road construction crew in southern Israel discovered an ancient synagogue near Kibbutz Nirim. Once the discovery is made, archaeologists excavate and reconstruct, but the initial discovery often belongs to the non-professional.

In 1929, an archaeological expedition "especially devoted to the clearance of Early Christian Churches"[7] found something at a site east of the Jordan River (modern Jerash), which they had *not* been looking for. Immediately under one of the churches, they found a synagogue. As the excavators themselves put it, "The discovery of a Jewish Synagogue . . . was . . . as unexpected as it was welcome."[8] One may question whether the archaeologists' surprise was entirely justified. Many synagogues no doubt still lie buried beneath the floors of old churches, and at least one other has already been discovered. At Jerash, much of the synagogue had actually been incorporated into the later church. The church itself was badly built and at first the archaeologists thought it was an inept reconstruction of

Jerash—Pairs of animals are either leaving or entering Noah's Ark. Upside down at the bottom is a Greek inscription with the remains of lions framing it. Beside the typical three-footed *menorah* are seen the usual incense shovel, *shofar* and *lulav* with *etrog*.

41

an earlier and better building which had been a pagan temple. However, when they dug beneath the floor, they found Hebrew inscriptions and the remains of a mosaic depicting the story of the biblical flood. The artistic quality of the mosaic places it among the finest ever to have been uncovered in a synagogue. Unfortunately very little of this artist's work has been preserved. The remains depict three rows of realistically rendered and easily identifiable animals entering or leaving Noah's ark. The mosaic also preserves the dove which Noah sent out from the ark after the earth had begun to recover from the forty days and forty nights of rain. The dove is sitting on a branch with a twig in its beak, ready to fly away from the ark.

We can only speculate as to the circumstances leading to the conversion of the building from a synagogue into a church, but the same sequence of events occurred many times during the Byzantine period.* The Jerash church is dated by an inscription to 530 C.E. The synagogue beneath it was probably built in the fifth century. It was almost certainly abandoned or destroyed during the anti-Jewish persecutions of the Emperor Justinian at the beginning of the sixth century.

If synagogues are to be found under churches, it will come as no surprise that they are also found under mosques. At ancient Shiloh, where the Ark of the Covenant rested from the time Joshua placed it there following the Israelite conquest of Canaan until it was later captured by the Philistines (see I Samuel 4:11), the Moslem residents hundreds of years ago built a commemorative mosque which is now in ruins. Mosaics are known to exist under the floor of the mosque. In the opinion of many scholars, these mosaics belong to an earlier synagogue.[10] Support for this theory comes from a fourteenth century traveller to the Holy Land, who reported that "Jews and Musselmans burn candles" there in memory of the fallen

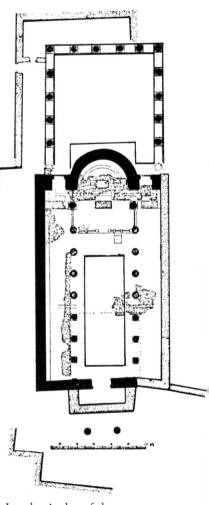

---

*What occurred during Byzantine times also occurred in the Roman period. According to literary records, Vespasian converted a synagogue into an *odeum* (a small, roofed theatre). At Daphne near Antioch he built an open air theatre on the site of a synagogue from the Jewish remains.[9]

shrine of Shiloh, which was once the central sanctuary of the Israelites.[11] Unfortunately the site has never been properly excavated. Perhaps some young reader of these pages will become the archaeologist to excavate this building and recover the ancient synagogue which still lies buried there.

Of course, without excavating, it is uncertain whether a building is a synagogue or not. But even when a building or its remains are completely exposed, doubt often persists. Consider the possibilities: A building might not be a synagogue, but a church, the early architecture of which often resembles the synagogue (and was probably influenced by it). Or the building might be a synagogue belonging not to Jews but to Samaritans, a sect which accepts as Holy Writ only Joshua and the Five Books of Moses and which broke away from Judaism after the Babylonian exile. A small group of Samaritans still maintains its ancient traditions in Israel today, but many more Samaritans inhabited the land in the early centuries of our era. Or a building might be a Judaeo-Christian synagogue-church from the time when many Christians regarded themselves also as Jews.[12] Or a building might have been a pagan temple, rather than a synagogue.

There are many kinds of indications to guide the scholar in his identification. Most of the time they are clear enough to leave little doubt. An orientation toward Jerusalem excludes a Samaritan synagogue. A *menorah* excludes a Christian church. An inscription that mentions an *archisynagogus* or a *hazzan* identifies a synagogue. And "Peace unto Israel" is just as good as proof.*

But sometimes the closest examination of the evidence still leaves the answer in doubt. The best scholars can change their minds—which is probably one reason they are the best.

The most famous case of mis-identification is the so-called Synagogue of Delos, located on one of the Greek isles in the Aegean Sea. Perhaps "famous" is the wrong word for this mis-identification, because even today, despite the fact that most scholars now have very serious reservations about this identification, thousands of tourists are shown the "Synagogue of Delos."[13]

A number of signs initially suggested to scholars that this building had been a synagogue. Built by the sea, it had probably been converted from a private home into a public building. It was apparently approached through a cluster of rooms with benches lining the walls and little evidence of internal decoration. What clinched the case were inscriptions carved on fragments of little columns. Each column was apparently placed in the building as a kind of offering of thanks in fulfillment of a vow, to express gratitude for recovery from illness. Several of the inscriptions which were in Greek had references to "God Most High"; one was offered "to the Most High." A typical inscription read: "Laodicus, to the God Most High, who cured him of his infirmities, *ex voto*". One of the inscriptions contained a Greek word (*proseuche*) which in some contexts is thought to mean synagogue. What more could be asked for? Even the most eminent of ancient synagogue scholars, E.L. Sukenik, considered the evidence sufficient to render the Jewish character of the building "almost certain."[14]

*As recently as 1975 a lovely mosaic was uncovered in Tel Aviv which reads in Greek, "Blessing and peace on Israel and on the place. Amen". This might be thought to identify the building as a synagogue. However, a companion mosaic in the Aramaic language is written in Samaritan script. This script indicates the building was probably a Samaritan synagogue, rather than a Jewish synagogue. (See "Notes and News", *Israel Exploration Journal*, Vol. XXVII, No. 1 (1977), p. 55)

Delos—One of the little votive columns which led archaeologist E. L. Sukenik to reject his earlier identification of the Delos building as a synagogue. On top of the columns, he found traces of lead apparently used to attach figurines to the top of the columns. This was surely not a form of Jewish offering, Sukenik concluded.

Nineteen years later, Sukenik reversed himself after he had an opportunity to examine the votive columns personally,[15] following a brilliant new evaluation of the Delos remains by a young scholar named Belle Mazur who argued persuasively that the Delos building was not a synagogue.[16] After a careful re-examination, the evidence that once seemed so strong proved deceptive. Inscriptions were found indicating that pagan Greeks referred to Zeus as the "God Most High"; so the reference on these Delos columns could as easily refer to Zeus as to the God of the Hebrews, argued Ms. Mazur. The Greek word which was thought to mean synagogue could also mean prayer—pagan prayer as well as Jewish prayer. According to Ms. Mazur, this sense appeared to fit the context far better here and was apparently what was originally intended. Moreover, a re-examination of the excavator's original report indicated that he himself seemed puzzled by a cache of clay oil-lamps. "It is curious to notice," he wrote, "that nothing in [the] decoration [of these lamps], testifies to any special adaptation to the clientele which used them. Some of them are even ornamented with motifs borrowed from paganism, a figure of Minerva, a bust of Jupiter."[17] Finally, Professor Sukenik observed on the top of the little offering columns the remains of lead which was apparently used to attach figurines to the top of the column. This form of the offerings was clearly pagan, not Jewish. So many scholars have now concluded that the building was probably not a synagogue, but a pagan shrine sacred to Zeus. However, boatloads of tourists are still carted off to see the "Delos Synagogue."

If buildings thought by scholars to be synagogues turn out not to be synagogues, the reverse is also true: sometimes a building is not recognized for the synagogue that in fact it is.

At the end of the last century, two German archaeologists excavated a building at Priene in Asia Minor which they identified as a church. They admitted being puzzled by a wall niche which had "only room for one priest."[18] Later archaeologists were able to identify the niche as a Torah receptacle. The identification of the building as a synagogue was clinched when E.L. Sukenik re-examined the excavation materials and found traces of two *menorot* on fragments inside the building.[19]

Many synagogue identifications are still in doubt. In the ancient city of Elche in southeastern Spain, a fourth-century building was excavated with characteristics of both a church and a synagogue. A mosaic inscription indicates a synagogue, but the choir is typical of a church. The building was excavated in 1905, and scholars are still arguing about its function. The most likely resolution of the matter is that the building was originally built as a synagogue but was later transformed into a church and reconstructed.[20]

More recently, the late Professor Michael Avi-Yonah of The Hebrew University of Jerusalem has suggested that a building at Mopsuestia in Syria, discovered in 1955 and identified by the excavators as a church, was in fact a synagogue.[21] Here was discovered a mosaic of Noah and the flood similar to the Jerash synagogue mosaic. Another series of mosaic panels at Mopsuestia tell the biblical story of Samson—the first time Samson appeared in church or synagogue art. The excavators date these mosaics from the end of the fourth or beginning of the fifth century, but, as Professor Avi-Yonah points out, this is quite late for biblical scenes to be used in the floor of a church, and the building may well be a synagogue.

One of the least known and least noticed ancient synagogues sits atop Mount Zion itself; it houses the *traditional* tomb of King David.* The holiness of the site—*because* it had once been a synagogue—helps explain why, beginning in the Middle Ages, this spot became known as the tomb of King David.

That the traditional tomb of King David is set in a building originally constructed as a synagogue was discovered only in 1949.[22] During the Israeli War of Independence, a shell exploded inside the room which housed the tomb. After the war, the room was examined and, to some extent, excavated prior to its repair. The Chief Inspector of the Department of Antiquities noted an apse behind the "sarcophagus" of David; this apse marked the building as a public structure. He measured the direction of the apse with a compass. It measured a few degrees east of north—*exactly* in

---

*Modern scholars all agree that the traditional site of the tomb of King David on Mount Zion is not, in fact, the actual tomb of King David. Modern archaeology has shown that the Jerusalem of King David's time was located on another ridge east of modern Mount Zion, known as the Ophel or City of David. This eastern ridge was the original Mount Zion or Fortress of Zion referred to in the Bible (II Samuel 5:7). Historically speaking, Zion has been a movable mountain. After David's time, the Temple Mount, the site of Solomon's Temple, became known as Mount Zion. By the turn of the era, Mount Zion had moved again, this time to Jerusalem's western ridge where it is now located. Why or how the change came about, we cannot be sure. Josephus, writing shortly after the destruction of the Second Temple, already refers to the western ridge of Jerusalem as David's Fortress. In the Middle Ages tradition placed King David's tomb here; the "sarcophagus" of King David now sits on a crusader floor. In the early part of the twentieth century a French archaeologist named Raymond Weill, the only Jew to excavate in Jerusalem prior to the establishment of the State of Israel, uncovered a necropolis on Jerusalem's eastern ridge where many scholars believe King David was probably buried.

the direction of the Temple Mount. He examined the walls and found that this apse was part of the original structure which could be dated to the late Roman period (c. 2d-3rd century C.E.). A niche in the wall of the apse, presumably for a Torah scroll, had its floor about 6 feet above the floor of the original room (the original floor of the room was found more than two feet below the present floor of the room). Similar niches at similar heights above the floor have been found at other ancient synagogues.

At a later stage, when the Moslems had conquered Jerusalem, a *mihrab* or prayer niche pointing to Mecca was built into the wall of the room opposite the apse. (Another wall, added by the Turks, now divides what was formerly one room into two, so the room with the *mihrab* now adjoins the room with the apse). At another stage in the building's history, a second story was added, which now houses a church of which the Coenaculum (the traditional site of Jesus' last supper) is a part. The church is oriented toward the east, as is customary in ancient churches.

Since the late Roman date of the apse in the original building precludes its use as a mosque or a church, it seems reasonable to conclude that the original building was a synagogue. This interpretation is confirmed by the orientation of the apse exactly toward the Temple Mount, just a few hundred yards away, in contrast to the later mosque which is oriented toward Mecca (south) and the church which is oriented to the east. The similarity of the niche in the apse to the niches in other synagogues also supports the identification of the building as a synagogue. Finally, this interpretation is consistent with the testimony of Epiphanius, a church father of the fourth century, who reports that there had been seven synagogues on Mount Zion, one of which had survived until his time.[23]

That the building had been a synagogue goes far toward explaining why this site became known, beginning in the Middle Ages, as the tomb of King David. By the Middle Ages, the building's earlier function was probably long forgotten; nevertheless, a certain holiness must have continued to adhere to this spot *because* it had been a synagogue. It is not difficult to understand how the suggestion arose that this holy site, pointing toward the Temple Mount and sitting on what was thought to be Mount Zion*, was King David's tomb. Eventually, the idea that this was King David's tomb took hold and became firmly entrenched until twentieth century archaeologists found that King David's Jerusalem was on another Jerusalem hill and that the traditional tomb-room of King David was a synagogue dating to the Roman period.

As recently as 1974 a synagogue now known as the Rehov synagogue was excavated in Israel's Beth Shean Valley. The excavation exposed a unique mosaic inscription—the largest mosaic inscription ever found in an ancient synagogue. It contains 29 lines of writing and about 365 words. The text concerns the laws of the sabbatical year and the tithing requirement as applied to areas of the country which produce different fruits and vegetables. The inscription contains lists of produce—melons, cucumbers and peas, figs, garlic and potatoes, bread, oil and wine, nuts, plums and sesame—as well as lists of cities—Beth Shean, Ashkelon, Acco, Dor and many more. It mentions Rabbi Judah the Prince and the King's mountain.**

---

*The Bible tells us that David was buried in the City of David, that is, within the city of Jerusalem as it existed in David's time (see I Kings 2:10).

**In the Talmud, the King's mountain refers to Jerusalem.

Rehov—The largest synagogue inscription ever discovered and the oldest extant copy of a part of the Talmud. The inscription measures 9 x 12 feet. The text relates to laws of the sabbatical year and requirements of tithing.

It discusses dispensations allowed during the sabbatical year and the separation of tithes in case of a doubt. The text appears to be a version of a portion of the Jerusalem Talmud and the *Tosephta*. This is the first time a passage from the Talmud has been found in a synagogue inscription. Dating from about the 6th century C.E., the inscription is the oldest extant copy of a talmudic passage, antedating other copies by many hundreds of years.

In recent years, newly accessible sites on the Golan Heights have revealed fragments of more than a dozen hitherto unknown ancient synagogues. At the Syrian military base at Quneitra, an inscribed column from an ancient synagogue was incorporated in a building. It read, "I, Yehuda the *hazzan* . . ." And so the search for ancient synagogues continues.

4 ✡ STYLES OF SYNAGOGUE ARCHITECTURE

*An overview of the kinds of
ancient synagogues*

In an earlier chapter, we examined what little is left of synagogues dating before the Roman destruction of the Temple in 70 C.E. After the destruction of Jerusalem, there is a hiatus in datable synagogue remains until about the end of the second century.

This is not surprising. The period was hardly conducive to the erection of prominent public Jewish buildings that would withstand the ravages of the centuries. The first Jewish revolt against the Romans, which culminated in Jerusalem's destruction, was followed some 60 years later by the second Jewish revolt, led by Rabbi Akiba and Bar-Kochba. Again the relatively small community of Jews was unsuccessful in defying the greatest temporal power the world had ever known. This time defeated Jerusalem was ploughed over and Jews were excluded not only from the Holy City, but from most of Judea. Many of Judea's Jews fled north to the Galilee where they reassembled in small rural communities. The Hadrianic persecutions which followed the Bar Kochba revolt led to the destruction, rather than the building of synagogues. Worshippers probably met in undistinguished buildings or private homes, and deliberately avoided calling attention to the places where they congregated.

Not until the end of the second century and the beginning of the third century, when emperors friendly to the Jews ruled in Rome, were public synagogues again constructed—or at least this is what scholars surmise from available evidence.[1] From this time until the eighth century, synagogues have survived throughout the length and breadth of the land—and in the diaspora as well. Although there were periods of Jewish persecution during this interval and even though the construction of new synagogues was forbidden by law beginning in the fifth century,[2] nevertheless synagogues were built and have survived throughout the period.

In the eighth century, following the Arab conquest of much of the then known world under the banner of Islam, there is another gap in datable

A bronze cuirass or body armor from a statue of the Roman emperor Hadrian recently found on an Israeli kibbutz. Hadrian suppressed the Second Jewish Revolt and banned Jews from Jerusalem. The decoration on the cuirass is a scene of victorious nude warriors and a defeated enemy kneeling in submission—the latter probably symbolizing vanquished Judea.

synagogue remains until the middle of the eleventh century. What emerges after this break is the medieval European synagogue which is beyond the scope of this book. With the rise of Islam, the period of the classical ancient synagogue in the Mediterranean world had come to an and. Our principal focus in this book will be on these ancient synagogues around the Mediterranean Sea dating from the third century to the eighth century C.E.— a period of 500 years.

During this frame of time we may distinguish three basic designs through which the history of the synagogue can be traced. By keeping in mind these three patterns, the reader will be able to organize much of the knowledge we have concerning the synagogues of this period.

The first is the so-called "basilica plan", the earliest design used for the classical synagogue, as shown here:

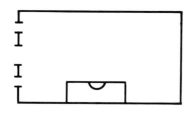

The basilica plan calls for a rectangular building with three doors—one large one and a smaller one on either side—in one of the short ends of the building. It has three rows of columns—on every side except on the side with the doorways. These three rows of columns divide the interior of the building into a central nave and three aisles—two on the sides and one in the back. Some of the most famous synagogue remains in the world follow this simple plan. The synagogue at Capernaum is one; Chorazim is another.

The second design is the so-called "broadhouse plan." This means simply that the building is broader than it is long. It looks like this:

The hallmark of this design is the Torah shrine in one of the long walls, which gives the building its orientation. Here was kept the holiest possession of Judaism—the scroll containing the Five Books of Moses. Like the basilica plan, some broadhouse plans have three doors in one of the short walls, as shown in the drawing; others have a door or doors in the long wall opposite the Torah shrine. Sometimes, the broadhouse synagogue is without columns though this is not invariably the case.

One of the most unusual synagogues in the ancient world follows the broadhouse design: Dura-Europos, in modern Syria. There are also ancient broadhouse-plan synagogues in present day Israel—for example in Eshtamoa and Sussiya.

The third principal synagogue design is the "apse plan," as shown here:

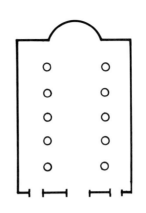

It too is a basilica, but an apse has been added in one of the short walls. The apse housed the Torah ark. Again we find three doors to enter the building—this time in the short wall opposite the apse. Instead of three rows of columns there are only two which create two interior aisles on either side of the apse. The synagogues with the most famous mosaic floors—Beth Alpha, Jericho and Aegina—all use this apse plan.

We omitted any mention of dates from this brief introduction to the three synagogue plans. The omission was deliberate for the question of dates is, as we shall see, a scholarly embarrassment. The dates given by excavators are often unreliable, and in a number of instances there is violent scholarly disagreement.

It is nevertheless true that a general, though not invariable, chronological pattern can be discerned. The earliest design by and large is the basilica-plan. Synagogues using this plan can probably be dated to the late second and third century C.E. and predominate in the Galilee. In the early fourth century the apse-plan first appears. Once it became established in the late fourth and fifth century, it was used continuously thereafter until the eighth century. Overlapping both the period of the basilica plan and the period of the apse plan was ths broadhouse plan, which has an uncertain relationship to what went before and what went after.

If all this seems confusing, it is confusing to scholars too. But it is better to accept the facts as they are than to attempt to force them into categories they don't fit.[3]

There are two curious—and not unrelated—aspects of the basilica plan. First, there is no structural feature for the placement of the Ark of the Law. In this respect, there is no "front" of the building; inside there is no permanent shrine to which attention is directed. The second noteworthy aspect of basilica-plan synagogues concerns their orientation with respect to the holy city of Jerusalem. The requirement that prayer—and therefore synagogues—be directed toward Jerusalem is traced to Solomon's great prayer at the dedication of the Temple (although, as we have seen in an earlier chapter, pre-destruction synagogues may have been oriented toward the east). Standing in front of the Altar of the Lord in the presence of the whole assembly of Israel, Solomon raised his hands toward heaven and prayed, "O Lord God of Israel, there is no god like thee in heaven above or on earth beneath . . . Hear the supplication of thy servant and of thy people Israel when they pray *toward this place.*"[4] Thus it is that in the diaspora, synagogues face Israel; in Israel synagogues face Jerusalem; and in Jerusalem synagogues face the Temple Mount where once stood the Holy of Holies.[5] Yet in basilica-plan synagogues, the front facade of the building—through which the building is entered—faces Jerusalem. Thus one who enters the building and faces the opposite wall will be oriented away from Jerusalem!

Scholars long puzzled over this paradox and finally came up with an explanation that not only accounts for the orientation of these early synagogues, but also explains the absence of any Torah shrine in basilica-plan synagogues. The basilica-plan synagogues originally had no permanent Torah shrine. Instead, they used a portable ark which was either carried or rolled in for the service, but was not kept in the main prayer-hall at other times. This portable ark—or possibly simply the scrolls themselves—was brought into the prayer hall through the large center door of the entrance facade during the service. In order to face this portable ark when it was brought in, the congregants would, on entering the synagogue and taking their place, turn around and face the door through which they had just come. In this attitude—facing the front facade—they directed their prayers toward Jerusalem and the Temple Mount. It has even been suggested that the large and ornately decorated center door of basilica-plan synagogues was used exclusively to bring in the Scrolls of the Law, the congregants themselves using the two smaller entrances on either side.

By contrast, in synagogues with a permanent Torah shrine built into the structure of the building, the Torah shrine, rather than the front facade of the building, faces Jerusalem.[6] When the apse plan became established, the apse faced Jerusalem. It was no longer necessary for congregants to turn around on entering the synagogue in order to face Jerusalem.

The theory of basilica-plan synagogues using a portable Torah ark also finds support in ancient talmudic and rabbinical sources, where we find a number of references to contemporaneous Torah shrines that were mobile.[7]

While broadhouse-plan synagogues all have a Torah shrine built into the structure of the building, some of these Torah shrines are little more than a niche or *aedicula*. Scholars have questioned just how the Torah was housed in these shrines. Many are too small for the Torah ark with panelled doors which we shall see so often represented in synagogues. Was the Torah simply placed in the niche? Did it have another kind of wooden housing which has by now disappeared? Was the Torah kept permanently in the Torah shrine or was it brought in just for the service? Was there a curtain covering the Torah or the Torah niche? There are no definitive answers to these questions.

Once the apse was adopted, we may assume that the wooden Ark of the Law, with its panelled doors capped by a pediment—as we shall see it again and again in these pages—was kept permanently in the apse.

Another difference between basilica-plan synagogues and apse-plan synagogues is that the floors of basilica-plans are paved with flagstones, apse-plans with mosaics. Broadhouse plans, as might be expected, are paved sometimes with one, sometimes with the other.

In this short introduction, we have discussed variations only in the basic plan of the synagogue room itself. Far greater variation can be seen in the construction of porticoes, annexes, siderooms, galleries, stairways and facades, to say nothing of variation in materials and decorations, both inside and out. So despite the fact that a basic typology may be used to describe the plans of ancient synagogues, the buildings themselves nevertheless vary greatly from one another, and reflect the creativity and imagination both of the architect and the craftsmen who carried out his design.

These synagogues were also buildings of their time reflecting the Graeco-Roman world of which they were a part. They changed in much the same way as other contemporaneous buildings which were not synagogues. Mosaics make their appearance in synagogues in the Byzantine period, just as mosaics became popular in churches and other public buildings at the same time. Synagogue architecture was a part of a larger culture, ultimately influencing it as well as being influenced by it. That synagogue buildings often looked like non-Jewish structures is reflected in the talmudic ruling as to what should be done to a Jew found bowing before a pagan temple, in the belief that it was a synagogue. The answer is, he is innocent.[8] The mistake, apparently, was understandable for the two buildings looked so much alike.

With this background, we can now examine more closely synagogues which use these three basic plans.

5 ✡ BASILICA-PLAN SYNAGOGUES

Mainly in the Galilee, heavily decorated in bas-relief on the outside

Basilica-plan synagogues are concentrated in the Galilee, in northern Israel, and in the adjacent Golan to the east. About twenty of these buildings have survived at least in part, although doubtless many more existed in times past and many more doubtless still exist beneath mounds of earth or other buildings, waiting to be discovered.

The strong similarity among these surviving synagogues suggests that they were built at about the same time, probably within two or three generations. When Hadrian expelled the Jews from Jerusalem and the surrounding area after the Bar Kochba revolt (135 C.E.), many Jews resettled in Galilee with the millennial hope that they could live out their lives in peace and freedom. If this was not to be their lot, it was given to their children, for toward the end of the second century C.E., a new attitude emanated from Rome. Later Antonine and Severan emperors were more tolerant of the Jews and their strange ways than any rulers the Jews had known for centuries. Most of the Hadrianic laws restricting Jews were repealed, and during the late second century and the third century, Jews appear to have flourished and prospered in dozens of small rural Galilean and Golan towns. Being free to do so, they built synagogues.

Over a century ago, the great French scholar, Ernest Renan discovered a dedicatory inscription from an ancient Galilean synagogue which reflects the amicable relations between the local Jewish community and the Roman emperor of the time. Severus, the emperor referred to in the inscription, reigned from 193 C.E. until 211 C.E. The inscription, which probably came from a basilica plan lintel reads as follows:

For the well-being of our Lord Autocrat Caesar Lucius Septimus Severus Pius Pertinax Augustus and . . . his son, by the vow of the Jews.

The tolerant and friendly attitude toward Jews reflected in this inscription

opposite
Archisynagogus was the mocking title given by his opponents to this Roman emperor, Alexander Severus, because of his tolerant attitude toward Jews.

55

also characterized other Severan rulers. Indeed, one of them, Alexander Severus, who reigned from 222 to 235, was so friendly to the Jews that his enemies referred to him as *"archisynagogus"*. So on historic grounds, this would seem to be a period when we might expect the Jewish community to be actively constructing synagogues.

The most beautiful and the best reconstructed of the Galilean basilica-plan synagogues is the famous synagogue of Capernaum, or Kfar Nahum, the village of Nahum, nestled on the shore of Lake Kinneret, the Sea of Galilee of the New Testament. In the midst of what must have been a lovely as well as prosperous Jewish community by the sea, the synagogue stands as a kind of town center.

The common building stone in this part of Galilee is a hard and durable rough black basalt; all the private buildings of Capernaum are built with it. The synagogue building alone is built of shimmering white limestone, highly polished to resemble marble. It indeed must have been an imposing structure—a white jewel in a black setting. Other Galilean communities,

56

Chorazim, for example, settled for black basalt for their synagogue as well as for their homes. But Capernaum was apparently wealthy enough to import the limestone from some distance.

But if the Capernaum villagers were prosperous, they were also practical people: they used the local black basalt for the foundations and white limestone only in the visible parts of the building. But on the visible parts they spared no expense; even the floor was paved with polished white lime flagstones.

The synagogue was entered by a flight of steps on either side of a platform which formed a walkway in front of the synagogue; the entire structure rested on a dais created with fill to raise the building above its surroundings. From the platform-walkway, three doors led into the synagogue proper. This entrance facade faced Jerusalem, as was typical before the introduction of a permanent Torah shrine inside the synagogue.

Above each of two smaller entrances was a small window; over the main entrance was a large semi-circular window which no doubt was the main source of light for the interior. Above that was another ornate window capped by a gabled roof and a so-called Syrian arch. Windows were customarily put in the Jerusalem facade, so light from the Holy City would shine on the worshippers. This tradition is supposedly based on a passage from the biblical book of Daniel: Following the famous edict that any subject who dared present a petition to any god or man other than the king would be thrown in the lion's pit, Daniel went home to pray. But before praying, he had windows which looked toward Jerusalem made in his room. Daniel's prayer was answered, and although he was thrown into the lion's pit, the lions did not harm him. So Jews traditionally place windows in the wall of their synagogues facing the Holy City. And thus it was at Capernaum.

Inside the synagogue two rows of stone benches, probably for the Elders, who governed the synagogue, lined the two long walls. The other congregants sat on mats on the floor in typically eastern fashion. Three rows of columns created three side aisles enclosing a central nave. The two corner columns had heart-shaped pedestals because they supported a

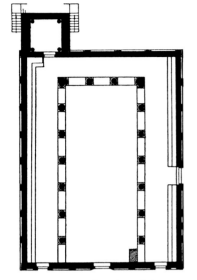

Capernaum—The plan of the synagogue. Benches line two walls of the synagogue. Corner columns are heart-shaped. To enter, one mounted stairs on either end of the platform in front of the structure. Behind the synagogue is a small room with stairs leading to a second-floor gallery, which might have been the women's entrance.

Capernaum—A reconstruction of the synagogue. The *beth ha-midrash* with its open courtyard is on the right. The synagogue, with its three entrances, is on the left. Note that the entire structure has been built on an artificial platform, approached by stairs on either side.

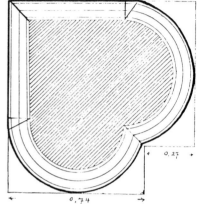

Capernaum A reconstruction of the interior of the synagogue showing the permanent Torah shrine which blocked the center entrance. Recent excavations have rejected this possible reconstruction of the Torah shrine.

Corner columns in Galilean and Golan synagogues were often heart-shaped as in this design of a corner column from Capernaum.

double column; one column supposedly came from each direction and met at the corner. If one were to look down onto one of these corner columns, it too would look heart-shaped, a design formed by two round columns coming together.

In its original state, the Capernaum synagogue had two stories. Above the two side aisles and supported by the interior columns was a gallery. Some of the smaller pillars which supported the roof of the gallery have been found in the excavations. The entrance to the gallery was by a separate outside stairway at the back of the building.

Until recently, it was assumed that this gallery overlooking the main

Capernaum—A reconstruction of the back of the synagogue showing the stairway to the second-floor gallery. Note the additional entrances to the *beth ha-midrash.*

opposite
Capernaum—Built of imported white limestone, the Capernaum synagogue is one of the most beautiful ancient synagogues in Israel.

Capernaum—This picture is important for what cannot be seen, rather than what is visible. This is the lintel of the main synagogue entrance. On either side of the lintel is a date palm affixed to a decorative scroll. At the top of the lintel is a series of wreaths. However, nothing holds the wreaths up. The little *erotes* or naked cupids that once held up the wreaths have been carefully chiselled out by an offended iconoclast. The wings of the cupids have not been completely defaced. They appear just inside the wreaths and were originally affixed to cupids that stood between the wreaths. At the bottom of the lintel was a spreadwing eagle—once the symbol of imperial Rome. The eagle too has been chiselled out, although the telltale remains identify it.

right
Capernaum—The pentagram or 5-pointed star, also known as the Seal of Solomon, is only one of several designs and objects enclosed in decorative circles. Neither it, nor the 6-pointed Magen David, which also appears in the Capernaum synagogue among a row of rosettes, had special Jewish significance at the time.

opposite
Capernaum—The decoration on the outside of the famous synagogue at Capernaum includes a carucca or Roman carriage carved in perspective: We see both the front and the side. What does it represent? The Ark of the Covenant? A portable Torah ark? The ark returning from its Philistine captives? No one knows for sure. The panelled doors and shell above resemble the doors of the ark pictured in numerous synagogue reliefs and mosaics.

61

Chorazim—This synagogue is built of local black basalt as were the other buildings of this Jewish Galilean town. The synagogue sits on a high hill above the Sea of Galilee which may be seen in the distance.

synagogue room was for women. Similar evidence of other second floor galleries in synagogues of the Capernaum-type, as well as other basic designs, has been discovered. Leading scholars found indications both in the Talmud and in Philo of the segregation of women during synagogue services; it was widely believed that this practice derived from the separation of the sexes in Herod's Temple as reflected in its "Women's Court",[1] especially since a separation of sexes was indubitably the case from medieval times to the present.

Like so many scholarly assumptions of the past, this theory too has been called into question in recent years. The Women's Court in the Temple, we are now told, was not for the exclusive use of women. The references in the Talmud and in Philo which supposedly reflect the separation of the sexes in early synagogues are inaccurately interpreted, based upon inference on inference, and gleaned from inauthentic texts. Recent scholarship has pointed out that despite the explicit law requiring women to pray and the frequent references to women attending synagogue services, there is no explicit statement, let alone law, that women were or must be segregated. And in the rabbinical descriptions of the synagogue, there is no reference to separation of the sexes. There is no reason to suppose that the galleries were for the exclusive use of women; many other uses can be hypothesized.[2]

If true, the fact that women were not segregated in ancient synagogues should provide some historical comfort to the present generation of Jewish women's liberationists, whose objection to sexual segregation would no doubt be compounded by the separate outside staircase at the back of the Capernaum synagogue to which scholars once consigned the ladies. The argument as to whether the women were separated from the men in ancient synagogues also provides fuel for the modern debate as to whether this separation is appropriate or required today. However, the usefulness of this scholarly material is limited by the fact that thus far neither side has yet been able to prove its position with a high degree of certainty.

Attached to one corner of the Capernaum building was a small room, which could be entered only from the synagogue. It was probably used for the storage of synagogue utensils and possibly even for Torah scrolls.

Beside the synagogue and attached to it was a colonnaded portico and court which, it has been suggested, was a *beth ha-midrash*; in effect, the community school. This school not only educated the children, but also provided an intensive program of what we would today call adult education. The room may also have been used for overnight accommodations for the ever present "needy stranger."

Fragments of another interior structure have also been found at Capernaum, but this does not appear on the synagogue plan. The remains of this structure were found inside the southern wall of the nave—adjacent to the central entrance to the synagogue.[2a] These fragments consist of various carved stones which many scholars are convinced were part of an elaborate Ark of the Law which was built in front of the main entrance to the Capernaum synagogue. A reconstruction of this ark, blocking the main entrance to the building, is shown in the illustration. This structure was not part of the original building but was added later to accommodate the Torah scrolls, which were then kept permanently in the main synagogue room. Obviously, after the installation of this interior structure, the synagogue could be entered only from the two side doors (or by the door from the annex).

In another Galilean basilica-plan synagogue (Bar'am), we can see from a

19th century engraving made from a very early photograph that the main entrance of the building was blocked by masonry while the two side doors were left open (see illustration). A picture of this same entrance taken around the turn of the century shows that some time between the two pic-

Bar'am—A 19th century engraving showing the blocked-up entrance of the center doorway of the synagogue. Perhaps the doorway was blocked up when a permanent Torah shrine was installed behind it.

tures, an enterprising local builder made off with the hewn-blocks which had been blocking the main center doorway. Some scholars believe that the masonry which blocked the main Bar'am doorway was part of the ancient structure, added when, as at Capernaum, a permanent Torah shrine was installed just inside the main entrance. Thus the case is gradually built for the introduction of a permanent Torah shrine sometime after the basilica-plan synagogues were originally constructed.

The Capernaum synagogue was richly decorated both inside and out, but especially on its exterior. The facade, the doorways, the windows, the columns, the capitals, the spaces between—all were heavily ornamented with running designs, rosettes, seashells, vines, leaves, garlands, bunches of grapes, scrolls and wreaths. Architectural fragments which now ring the site abundantly testify to what the synagogue must have looked like in its original state.

Bar'am—The center doorway of the synagogue as seen today.

Among the decorations are a number of specifically Jewish symbols, although their occurrence is not frequent considering the amount of ornamentation on the building. A *menorah,* the seven-branched candelabra from the Temple, sits atop the acanthus leaves on the capital of a column.[3] On one side of the *menorah* is a *shofar* and on the other an incense shovel, also recalling the days when the Temple was still functioning. A palm tree with two bunches of dates served as a support on either side of the lintel over the main doorway. For both Jews and gentiles of the time, the palm tree was a symbol of Judea and Jewry. Elsewhere on the building, a palm branch or *lulav,* used on the festival of *Succot,* is carved in low-relief.

Another Jewish symbol which adorned the building was a representation of the Ark of the Law. This appeared in the center of the lintel over

the door to the annex which, as we have noted, probably housed the *beth ha-midrash*. As we shall see, in later synagogues the Ark of the Law pictured much like this will become a common decoration, but this is one of its first synagogue appearances, surprisingly enough at a time when the wooden Ark of the Law was not yet permanently housed inside the prayer hall. Apparently at a very early date the basic design of the Torah ark was established: two panelled doors capped by a pediment. Is this a depiction of the wooden Ark of the Law that was carried in for the service? Or is it supposed to be a depiction of the Ark of the Law that existed in the days of the First Temple? Perhaps it was both.

Another relief carving which presents difficulties of interpretation is the so-called "carucca" or wheeled carriage which appears twice in the carvings at Capernaum. A carucca was a Roman carriage for high-ranking officials, but it is difficult to believe that this was what the synagogue relief intended to depict here. Some scholars have suggested that it is supposed to be a representation of the portable Ark of the Law or the Ark of the Covenant which the ancient Hebrews carried through the desert until it found its permanent home in the Jerusalem Temple. Of course, according to this interpretation, the portable ark is seen through the eyes of Jews who have been heavily influenced by Graeco-Roman culture. Note, for example, the five ionic columns on the side of the carriage, which we are able to see because the carriage is drawn in perspective—one of its many unusual features. The front of the shrine contains the standard panel doors and is topped by a pedimental shell.

Other scholars suggest that this carriage depicts the portable shrine that was rolled into the synagogue for the service before a permanent Torah shrine became part of the structure of the building. Note that there is

Capernaum—A typical frieze from the synagogue's richly decorated interior. The wavy six-pointed star (third from left) is given no more prominence than the variety of rosettes and fruit in other circles.

no indication that the carriage was drawn by animals. Still other scholars believe that the carriage is a Romanized representation of the mystic chariot mentioned in one of Ezekiel's visions (Ezekiel 1:18-21). Unfortunately, none of these explanations seems more convincing than the others.

Several friezes in the Capernaum synagogue also depict six-pointed and five-pointed stars. The six-pointed star, or hexagram, is the well-known *Magen David* or Shield of David, one of the most popular modern Jewish symbols. Lesser known as a Jewish symbol is the five-pointed star, or pentagram, which is sometimes referred to as the Seal of Solomon. The thrill of recognition with which many tourists greet this early appearance of the *Magen David* is unfortunately unjustified. Scholars tell us that the *Magen David* did not emerge as a Jewish symbol until the Middle Ages, when it

was used as a magical amulet to ward off evil spirits. Even then it was not a popular design. Only in the nineteenth century was the *Magen David* widely adopted as a symbol for Judaism generally—on the walls and roofs of synagogues, on tombstones, and on sacred objects of all kinds. However, as one scholar has put it, "The prime motive behind the wide diffusion of the sign . . . was the desire to imitate Christianity. The Jews looked for a striking and simple sign which would 'symbolize' Judaism in the same way as the cross symbolizes Christianity."[4] Then in 1897 the *Magen David* was adopted as the Zionist emblem and became the central design on the Zionist flag. Despite its late appearance, the *Magen David* became hallowed as a Jewish symbol when it was worn by the six million Jews who perished in Hitler's crematoria. Subsequently, the Zionist flag with its *Magen David* became the flag of the reborn State of Israel. However, when the new state chose its emblem, it reached back to an older tradition, as we shall see in these pages, and chose instead the *menorah*, the seven-branched candelabra from the destroyed Temple.

The six-pointed star as a geometric design has been found as early as the Bronze Age (3200 B.C.E.-1200 B.C.E.) and in civilizations as widely separated as Mesopotamia and Britain. In the Iron Age (1200 B.C.E.-586 B.C.E.), examples have been found all the way from India to the Iberian peninsula. Given this history, we should not be surprised to see the hexagram on early Jewish artifacts from time to time. However, we have no reason to suppose that it was anything more than a pleasing geometric decoration at the time. At Capernaum, this is confirmed by the fact that the hexagram is part of a frieze which includes a number of designs—the pentagram, rosettes of various kinds and other decorations. No one of these designs is given more prominence than another, and it is no more likely that the hexagram was intended as a specifically Jewish symbol than that the rosette which sits beside it was so intended.

A description of the ornamentation of the Capernaum synagogue would not be complete without mention of those things which cannot be seen, or can be dimly seen at best. In short, an iconoclast has been at work; wherever he found the "likeness of anything in the heavens above, or on the earth below, or in the waters under the earth," he destroyed it with his chisel. Fortunately, he did his work carefully, with obvious respect for the building itself. Only the offending image was chiselled out; everything else was neatly—even painstakingly—preserved.

In most cases, we can even discern in outline what had been there before. The destroyed images fall into two classes. The first class consists of animals—mostly lions and eagles with spread wings. The spread-wing eagle can still be dimly seen in the lintel over the main doorway of the synagogue. Ironically enough, a few hundred years before, when Herod placed a spread-wing Roman eagle over the door of the Jerusalem Temple, this almost started a Jewish insurrection. But by the time the Jews built their synagogue at Kfar Nahum, times had changed. Apparently there was no objection then to the eagle over the main entrance to the synagogue building; indeed, the Jews chose it themselves. However, attitudes would change again and then the iconoclast would wield his chisel, carefully removing all but the outline of all living things.

Animals were not the only images that crumbled under the iconoclast's chisel at Capernaum. The synagogue's original ornamentation also included human forms taken from Roman mythology. Look more closely at the lintel that once graced the main entrance to the synagogue. Above the spot where the eagle was removed is a row of garland wreaths forming five semi-circles, a rosette within each. We know this pattern from innumerable classical sources. We also know that the garlands are often held up by someone; they did not hang in mid-air. A careful examination of the lintel will reveal that these garlands were at one time indeed upheld—by the usual graceful naked winged cupids (*erotes* in Greek), one on either end of the row and one between each of the garland wreaths. Although the heads and bodies of these *erotes* have been completely chiselled away, traces of their outspread wings can still be discerned. Elsewhere on the building, the iconoclast has removed a leaping centaur and possibly other mythological figures.

It is too early in our survey to consider the twists and turns of the Jewish attitude toward the representation of animals and human forms on their synagogues. Later in these pages, we will also consider what meaning, if any, these Graeco-Roman symbols held for the Jewish community that used them to decorate their houses of prayer. Suffice it to say here that these symbols appear even on the earliest synagogues after the destruction of the Temple, like Capernaum.

Although the precise date of the Capernaum synagogue is uncertain, the end of the second century or first part of the third century appears to be the most likely date. However, while this dating is accepted by the majority of scholars, a number of others have argued for different dates ranging from the first century to the fourth or fifth century. The argument for the earlier date—the first century C.E.—is perhaps unavoidably bound up with the references in the New Testament to the Capernaum synagogue. Shortly after John the Baptist baptized Jesus in the River Jordan, Jesus settled in Capernaum, and this became the center of his ministry until he left for Jerusalem. The Gospel refers to Capernaum as Jesus' "own town." More specifically, the Gospels tell us that Jesus preached and taught frequently in the Capernaum synagogue and performed a number of miraculous cures there. It was in the Capernaum synagogue that Jesus uttered the famous mystical words that so outraged his fellow Jews and which have since become a cornerstone of Catholicism: "Whoever eats my flesh and drinks my blood possesses eternal life, and I will raise him up on the last day. My flesh is real food; my blood is real drink . . . As the living Father sent me . . ., he who eats me shall live because of me. This is the bread which came down from heaven" (John 6:53-58). Thus the word of Jesus went forth first from Capernaum.

The natural predilection of early Christian scholars to date the Capernaum synagogue to Jesus' time was given a significant boost by a man who devoted the greater part of his professional life to the study and restoration of Capernaum. Friar Gaudentius Orfali supervised the Franciscans' archaeological work at Capernaum from 1921 until 1926 when he was tragically killed in an automobile accident. He is memorialized in an inscription on one of the Capernaum synagogue pillars. (Two ancient inscriptions are also inscribed on these columns, one in Aramaic and one in Greek, commemorating donations to the synagogue for the erection of columns). The results of Fr. Orfali's labors were published shortly before his death in a beautiful book entitled *Capharnaum et Ses Ruines*.[5] In it Fr. Orfali argues that the synagogue was already in existence in the early first century C.E. Accordingly, this was the same building in which Jesus preached and performed his miracles. However, the arguments Fr. Orfali has adduced to support this early date have been characterized by other leading scholars as "unconvincing"[6] "improbable"[7] and even "superficial."[8] This judgment is supported by the fact that Fr. Orfali has been the only modern scholar to advance such an early date for the Capernaum synagogue. It is of course possible that the Capernaum synagogue referred to in the New Testament was located on the same spot as the present remains. Recently, traces of an earlier building have been found below the present building. One eminent Israeli scholar has suggested that this earlier building was too large and well-paved to be anything but a public building and may well have been an earlier synagogue.[9]

In 1968 the Franciscan Fathers renewed their excavations of the Capernaum synagogue and this time, to the surprise of everyone including themselves, they concluded that the present synagogue building dates from some time between the last decade of the fourth century and the middle of the fifth century. This finding has precipitated one of the liveliest debates the scholarly world of synagogue archaeology has witnessed in a long time. The Italian excavators are arrayed on one side and leading Israeli scholars on the other. However, instead of the two-fisted slugfest that usually characterizes Israeli scholarly debate, the current disagreement between the Italian scholars and the Israelis has proceeded with almost diplomatic politeness.

The debate is interesting because it illustrates how deucedly difficult it is to interpret archaeological materials. The crux of the Italian position rests on coins, numbering more than 10,000, found under the pavement of

Capernaum—An interior view of the synagogue showing the back row of columns. A modern inscription to the memory of Friar Orfali can be seen engraved on the second column from the left. Part of the flagstone pavement of the synagogue is also visible.

the present synagogue building. As we have already noted the present synagogue building was constructed on a platform created by the use of fill in order to give the structure a more monumental appearance. According to the Italians, a thick layer of mortar was laid on top of this fill, and the synagogue pavement was laid on top of the mortar. The Italian excavators found their coins in the fill and in the mortar which, they claim, sealed the fill below it. Some of the coins were actually embedded in the mortar. These coins have been dated to the fourth and fifth centuries and, according to the Italians, require them to date the synagogue building to the same period.[10]

The Israelis, on the other hand, emphasize the artistic and stylistic parallels to the Capernaum building which clearly point to the end of the second or third century for its construction.[11] The Israelis also emphasize the unacceptable consequences that would flow from a late dating of the Capernaum building. For example, the Capernaum synagogue then would be contemporaneous with an entirely different kind of synagogue structure at Hammath-Tiberias, only a few miles away. Were these buildings in fact contemporaneous, "we would probably find this to be the only case of such astounding architectural diversity within so small an area," says Hebrew University Professor Michael Avi-Yonah.[12] Moreover, barely 30 feet from the Capernaum synagogue the Italian excavators themselves place a modest house (which they believe was St. Peter's) that was transformed and used as a church in the fourth century. Can we accept the fact that so magnificent and richly decorated a synagogue as Capernaum would be allowed to be built so close to a church whose religion was now the state religion. As one Israeli scholar has commented, "Such a state of affairs might be conceivable in our ecumenical age, but it seems impossible to imagine that it would have been allowed by the Byzantine authorities of the fourth century."[13] No doubt, there were synagogues built in the fourth century (probably as a result of bribes to local officials because Byzantine law at the time forbade the erection of new synagogues), but all their splendor was reserved for the interior, not flaunted on the exterior to proclaim the violation of the emperor's law.

For all of these reasons, the majority of Israeli scholars have adhered to the second-third century dating for the Galilean basilica-plan synagogues, including Capernaum.

But what of the coins "hermetically sealed,"[14] as the Italian excavators put it, under the synagogue pavement? How did these coins dating from the fourth and fifth centuries get under the floor of a second or third century building? Perhaps, say the Israelis, the pavement was relaid in the fourth century at which time a fill could have been spread inside the building and a layer of mortar placed over it.[15]

The Italians reply, "We found no hint anywhere that the stone pavement was rebuilt; one claiming that such rebuilding took place would have to prove his theory."[16]

The Israelis cannot "prove their theory," at least to the Italians' satisfaction. All they can do is charge the Italians with an "overly confident use of the term 'hermetically sealed' [to describe the levels under the synagogue pavement]. No sealing in an ancient site was ever 'hermetic' in the physical sense."[17]

Thus the debate goes on. What the resolution will be, no one can tell for sure. But most scholars privately believe that ultimately the Israeli dating of Capernaum will prevail.

On the other hand, if the Italian excavators prove correct and a date in the late fourth or early fifth century is established for the Capernaum synagogue, this will require a re-dating of the approximately 20 similar structures scattered throughout the Galilee. This in turn will require a thorough re-writing of the history of the Jews in Palestine during the fourth and fifth centuries. As we know this period today, it was one of persecution and decay, a time when Jews emigrated from the Holy Land instead of coming to it. A dating of Capernaum and the other basilica-plan synagogues to the fourth and fifth centuries would indicate that this was instead a period of prosperity and vigor, a time when Jewish life flourished, rather than decayed.

For the Israelis, the historical conditions in Palestine in the fourth and fifth centuries are another reason why the Italians must be wrong. But, if the Italians are right and the history of the period is re-written, it will not be the first time that archaeology has required us to modify our views of the past. These then are the stakes in the argument—which helps to explain not only why this scholarly debate is so fascinating, but also why it is so important.

The Capernaum synagogue has been described in such detail, not only because it is the most beautiful and best preserved basilica-plan synagogue structure,[18] but also because its features are repeated again and again in other synagogues of the period—the basic shape and column arrangement of the prayer room, details such as the heart-shaped corner columns, the three doors in the entrance facade which faces Jerusalem, the windows and design of the facade, the absence of a permanent niche for the Torah ark, as well as the pattern of the ornamentation—heavier on the outside than on the inside and with the same motifs, both Jewish and non-Jewish. Even the iconoclastic destruction of some of the same images is part of a repeated pattern. In hardly a detail is Capernaum unique.

That is not to say that we do not find variations in basilica-plan synagogues. The amount of ornamentation varies from synagogue to synagogue, some plainer than others. At Meiron, there is almost a complete absence of decoration, either because the congregation was poor or because it adhered to a stricter interpretation of the prohibition against images. Frequently, basilica-plan synagogues contain no specifically Jewish symbols; this may be because they have been carried away rather than because they never existed. Sometimes the iconoclast did his work less thoroughly or failed to make an appearance at all. For example, at Chorazim a head of Medusa is preserved, as well as a sculptured lion's head and a frieze of a wine-making ceremony in which the vintners are happily treading grapes.[19]

Even the plan of the synagogue varies within the basic basilica style. Frequently, the annex or the storage room is missing. Occasionally the entrance to the building is by a single central door. The Bar'am synagogue—which, incidentally, is the only basilica-plan facade preserved to the second story—not only has the usual three entrances in the facade, but also has a

Chorazim—The head of Medusa, as portrayed in the synagogue. According to Greek mythology, Medusa had snakes for hair; she was slain by Perseus who presented her head to the goddess Athena.

73

Bar'am—The only basilica-plan synagogue facade that has been preserved to the second story.

Bar'am—A reconstruction of the synagogue with its handsome and unusual entrance portico.

covered portico. in front of it.

The orientation of the synagogue may be altered to fit the requirements of an unusual site, and naturally the fine polished limestone of the wealthy Capernaum synagogue is not the rule. Just three miles to the north of Ca-

Meiron—The facade of the synagogue, shown here, faces south. It is the longest of the Galilean synagogues, but not by much. The portals are without decoration. We do not know whether this was for economic reasons, religious reasons, or because of design preference. In any event, it contrasts sharply with the heavily decorated facade of Galilean synagogues like Capernaum. The right portal has been reconstructed.

pernaum at Chorazim, we can see a synagogue wholly constructed of the local black basalt.

Another variation in basilica-plan synagogues concerns their location. According to the *Tosephta*, the synagogue should be built on the highest ground in the town; any house whose roof was higher than the synagogue would end in destruction.* However, already in Josephus, another tradition is recorded; when possible, the synagogue should be located beside a body of water: the sea, a lake or a river. The Capernaum synagogue appears to follow this tradition (although as we have seen, the builders of the Capernaum synagogue attempted to give it additional height by constructing it on an artificial platform, and its second story no doubt made it the highest building in town). Other basilica-plan synagogues, following the talmudic prescription, command a breathtaking view of the hills of Galilee which rise on either side of the lake.

But all of those variations are small compared to the similarities and only serve to emphasize the common features which unite these early basilica-plan synagogues.

opposite top
Gush Halav—This synagogue in northern Galilee is shown literally coming out of the ground. It has been only partially excavated, as may be seen from the ground line on the right. It is located amidst a grove of fig trees. The Galilean hills can be seen in the background.

opposite right
Gamla—This recently excavated building on the Golan Heights dates from before the destruction of the Temple in 70 C.E. Gamla was a well-known Jewish town destroyed by the Romans in 67 C.E. during the first year of the Jewish revolt. The building shown here had columns and benches like the later Galilean synagogues. Is it too a synagogue? Many scholars believe it is, although no clear archaeological proof has yet been found. But if it isn't a synagogue, what is it? If it *is* a synagogue, it is the first synagogue building from a Jewish town which pre-dates the destruction of the Temple.

opposite left
Gamla—A heart-shaped column reminiscent of later Galilean synagogues like Capernaum.

*In the Middle Ages, many a synagogue had a pole on the roof technically to comply with the admonition that the synagogue should be the highest building in town.

6 ✡ DURA-EUROPOS

Window into a vanished Jewish world

The time is 255 C.E., give or take a year or two.[1] The place is a Roman garrison town on the western bank of the middle Euphrates, about half way between Baghdad and Aleppo. In 255 C.E., the place is called Europos. But old timers call it Dura, the Assyrian name by which the town was called when founded hundreds of years ago. Since then the town has changed hands many times—and names too. When it fell to the Seleucids after the death of Alexander the Great in 323 B.C.E., the new dynasty renamed it Europos, after the little town in Macedonia where Seleucus himself had been born. Later, when the Parthians from Iran became rulers of the city, they changed its name back to Dura. Then the Roman emperor Trajan captured it, but failed to hold it long enough to give it another name. A hundred years later a second Roman conquest proved more lasting, and the name again became Europos. To avoid confusion, twentieth century scholars refer to the town as Dura-Europos.

In 255 C.E. Dura-Europos is a Roman garrison town on the eastern *limes*, that plural-sounding singular word by which the Romans called their fortified frontier. Once, Dura-Europos was a caravan city of some importance, for it lies on that ancient route over which caravans plied the western bank of the Euphrates River for centuries. After the Romans pacified the desert, the route shifted south. But Dura-Europos remained a military center, and the size of the Roman garrison keeps the town prosperous.

No one knows for sure how long the Jews have been here. But they have had a synagogue for at least 50 or 75 years, not the new one that was roofed over just 10 years ago, in 245 C.E., but an earlier building on the same site. Although their numbers are not large, the Jews are among the more prominent groups in town.[2] They live together in a few blocks clustered around their new synagogue on the western side of the city, next to the city wall. Despite their strange ways, the Roman soldiers like them, and the Jews have prospered.

The leader of the Jewish community is Samuel, the Elder, the priest, the *kohen*, the head of the synagogue. It was he who directed the building of the new synagogue. His name is inscribed on the beautiful tiles in the ceiling.

We do not know who brought the word to Samuel, but someone from the Roman garrison must have been sent to tell the Jewish leader that his synagogue—and, indeed, the entire Jewish quarter—was to be requisitioned for a new defense fortification against a probable Sassanian siege.

Whoever brought the message rode first through the straight well-laid-out streets of the town until he came to the Jewish quarter. An alley off the street led to the synagogue compound; a stranger would have difficulty finding the way.

First left, then right, then left, through the halls and courts of what had once been a private home. When the new synagogue was built to replace the old one, the house in front was converted for adjunct synagogue use—as rooms for Jewish travellers to spend the night, rooms for young Jews to study in, rooms to store synagogue books and utensils, and even apartments for synagogue officials.

When the messenger reached Samuel's apartment, he no doubt explained that not only the Jews' quarter, but the entire area along the western wall of the town was being requisitioned. Everyone knew that the attack would come from the west. It was the time-honored direction; it was the only feasible way. Dura-Europos was built on a high plateau overlooking the Euphrates River. On the east is a sheer drop, down to the river. But on the west is the Syrian desert. The attacker would, as always, march up the west bank of the Euphrates, along the ancient trade route, then curve around to the west, turn and approach the plateau on which the city stands.

The Roman defense plan was ambitious. Inside the western wall of the city was a street; the plan was to fill up this street to add to the thickness of the city wall. The city wall could withstand the pressure of the fill, but the building walls on the other side of the street could not. A supporting ramp on the other side of the building walls would have to be built—which

79

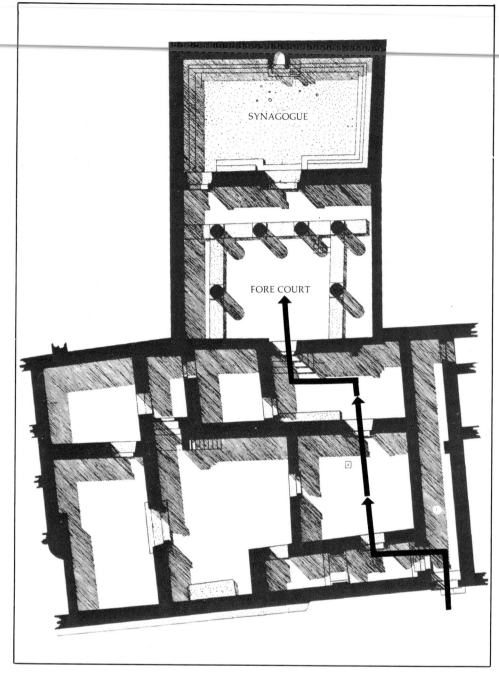

SYNAGOGUE

FORE COURT

Dura-Europos—A plan of the synagogue, the forecourt, and some private rooms in front. The only entrance to the complex is through the alley-like passage in the lower right. The back wall of the synagogue, where the Torah niche is located, faces on Wall Street. Note the benches lining the walls, and two entrances—a larger one opposite the Torah niche and a smaller one, perhaps for women, on the left.

required the destruction of the buildings.

The plan was sensible, even ingenious. No one could quarrel with it. And it also made sense to get on with the job as quickly as possible. Everyone seemed to be aware that the Roman Empire was gradually losing its vitality. Even an outpost like Dura-Europos had heard of the growing political anarchy that enveloped imperial Rome. Morever, a new Persian dynasty, the Sassanians, had recently become heir to Parthian Persia. More aggressive than the last Parthian rulers, the Sassanians seemed determined to relieve Rome of its eastern provinces. The Sassanians had already attempted one unsuccessful siege of the city. Another was almost inevitable. Perhaps they would succeed the second time.

The Jewish quarter borders on what has become known as Wall Street, the street just inside the city wall. The back of the western wall of the synagogue—the Jerusalem wall—faces Wall Street.

Dura-Europos—A plan of the city. The straight wall on the left faces the desert. In this wall is the main gate to the city. The upper right side of the city needed no wall, since it is situated on a cliff overlooking the Euphrates River. The synagogue is located in the second square to the left of the main gate (L-7 on the plan). The back of the synagogue faces directly on Wall Street—the street just inside the wall and running parallel to it. The city is well laid out in neat, rectangular city blocks.

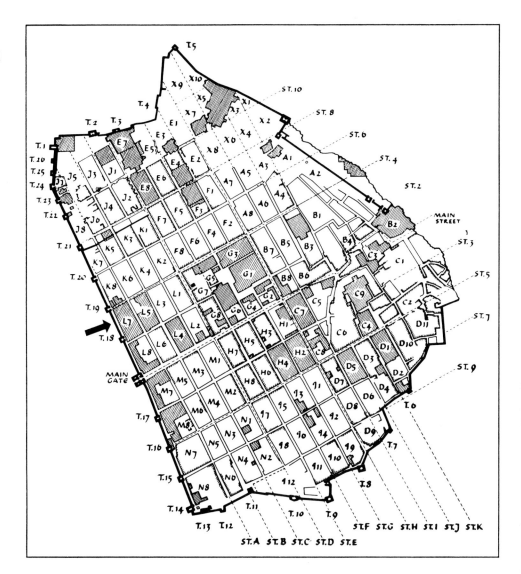

In front of the synagogue is a large colonnaded forecourt which provides an impressive entrance to the synagogue. A visitor would cross this forecourt and then enter the synagogue.

The synagogue room is not large as public buildings go, but still it is one of the largest in all of Dura-Europos. It is 42 feet wide and just over half that size in length. The Torah shrine, a niche or *aedicula*, is built into the center of one of the long walls, opposite the main door of the columnless room. At the end of the long wall with the main door in it is a small door. (Excavators 1700 years later will tell us this door is for the women—who sit in the corner of the room. The excavators will not be able to say whether a screen divided the women from the men.) The comfortable footrests that accompany the two rows of benches that line the walls are absent in the women's section, which is near the so-called women's entrance.[3] Feminine modesty and propriety do not permit the women—even with their long dresses—to raise their feet like the men. The benches accommodate 124 people. Many more can sit on the rugs which cover the floor. The ceiling is high—over 20 feet—and gives the room a feeling of spaciousness and spirituality. Light streams through small windows in the walls just below the ceiling.

Heavy wooden beams divide the ceiling in thirds and square tiles line the spaces between the beams. A pair of these inscribed tiles contains Samuel's

But there is no postponing the inevitable. The Jews evacuate their homes and their synagogue; Roman workmen begin filling up the street (which lies between the western town wall and the synagogue) with dirt and sand. At the same time, the western wall of the synagogue, the wall which contains the shrine for the Torah (the Torah having been removed) is buttressed by an embankment of earth and carefully packed mud. The earth and mud embankment inside the synagogue runs almost from the ceiling of the western wall to the middle of the floor. Then the filling of the street is completed—almost to the level of the housetops.

In the course of these preparations for the siege, the western wall of the synagogue is cracked and pushed in at the middle and the top. But it hardly matters; the building cannot be used ever again.

Next, more layers of fill are placed on both sides of the city wall. On the inside of the wall, the embankment now slopes down to the far side of the synagogue room and into the forecourt. Then those parts of the walls of the synagogue which project above the sloping embankment are demolished. The Jewish houses beyond the embankment are also razed to create an open defense zone inside the now heavily embanked city wall. Thus the setting is prepared for hand-to-hand combat inside the city should the defense of the walls fail.

Sometime within the next two or three years, surely no later than 260 C.E., the Sassanian siege came. Despite the enormous effort to bolster the city's defenses, Dura-Europos was captured and sacked.

The fate of the Jewish community of Dura-Europos is not recorded. We may assume that they shared the fate of other members of the community; those who were unable to escape were massacred or sold into slavery.

The town itself was occupied for a short time by the Sassanians and then abandoned to time and the desert. Gradually all was covered with sand and Dura-Europos disappeared from history for seventeen centuries.

The scene shifts to 1921 C.E. Fighting again rages on the site of Dura-Europos. The combatants this time are the British and the Arabs. The British are expecting an Arab attack from the Syrian desert, just as the Romans did. However, the British defense strategy is different. The British commander orders his men to dig trenches in the sand. In the course of the digging, the soldiers come upon some paintings from a pagan temple of some Palmyrene gods. The scholarly world is alerted.

Between 1928 and 1937, ten archaeological campaigns are conducted at Dura-Europos. In the course of these excavations, the ancient synagogue is discovered. The earth fill which the Romans had placed in the synagogue miraculously served as a preservative. Some of the paintings look as if they had been painted a month before.

Let us listen to one of the excavators describe the moment:

The work in other trenches [except the synagogue] almost stopped! Members of the expedition, not already there, were hastily summoned. It was a scene like a dream! In the infinite space of clear blue sky and bare gray desert, there was a miracle taking place, an oasis of painting springing up from the dull earth. The size of the room was dwarfed by the limitless horizons but no one could deny the extraordinary array of figures, the brilliant scenes, the astounding colors. What did it mean? [3a]

Unfortunately, the brilliant colors become dull even within the time it takes the archaeologists to remove the bits of dust and earth which cling to the surface. The brilliance of the colors is restored when the archaeologists

Dura-Europos—Four stages in the construction of the ramp built to defend the city against a Persian assault. These are section drawings—a vertical slice of the city extending from the city wall on the right to a private room in front of the synagogue on the left. Reading from right to left, the first vertical black line is the city wall inside a turret which protrudes from either side of the wall, more on the outside than on the inside. Inside the wall is Wall Street. On the other side of Wall Street is the back wall of the synagogue where the Torah niche can be seen. In front of the synagogue, is the columned forecourt. In front of the forecourt is a private building. The first section drawing shows the fill in Wall Street to the height of the Torah niche. The second section drawing shows Wall Street filled up almost to the height of the synagogue ceiling, with a glacis on the outside of the wall and the inside of the synagogue. The third section drawing shows the addition of more fill to create a ramp on the inside of the city and a steep glacis outside; by this time, the synagogue wall has cracked and bent under the pressure. In the fourth section drawing the ramp has been completed and all buildings protruding above it have been removed.

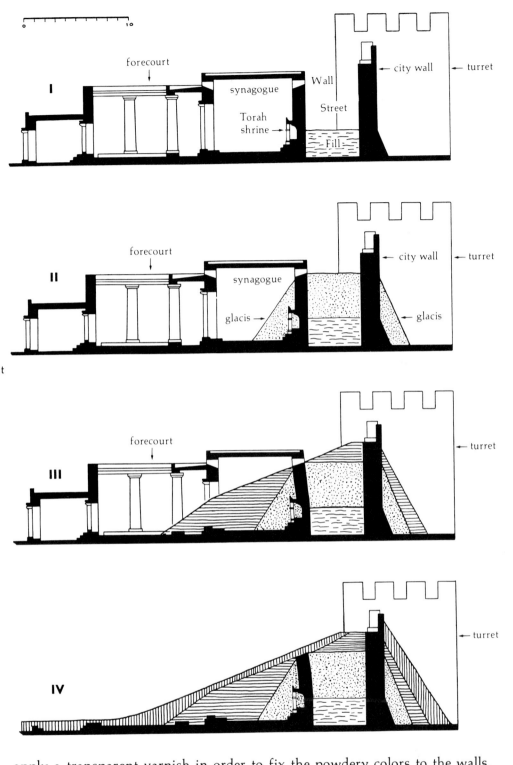

apply a transparent varnish in order to fix the powdery colors to the walls. But as the varnish dries, the colors again lose that fresh lively look, much the same way mosiacs become brilliant when washed with water and then return to their more somber colors as the water evaporates.

The parts of the walls which projected above the embankment are destroyed, as is almost all of the eastern wall. But the western wall, with the beautiful Torah shrine, is almost completely recovered. The two side walls show the sloping line of the embankment rising from east to west. The paintings below this sloping line are preserved; above, everything is gone. In all, about half the paintings that once covered the walls of the syna-

Let us look at a few of these pictures more closely, recognizing that at best we can but skim. E. R. Goodenough, for example, devoted three folio volumes just to their Jewish symbols.

Most of the better preserved pictures are on the west wall where the Torah shrine is located. For it was this wall that was most completely covered by the mud embankment. Immediately to the left of the Torah shrine, on the lowest of the three registers, is a panel from the Book of Esther, read in the synagogue on the festival of *Purim*. The Book of Esther is a legendary story of how the Jewish people were saved from the evil Haman by Mordecai and his beautiful ward Esther, who became queen to the Persian king. The limits of the panel are marked by a strip of border decorated with a wavy line. Within the panel are actually three scenes, although there is no division between them. On the left is Mordecai in regal dress sitting on a white steed, with the humiliated Haman as his groom, leading Mordecai's horse; on the right is King Ahasuerus, sitting on a golden throne with his wife Queen Esther beside him; in the center is a group of four men whose identity is a mystery.

There can be no question about the identity of Mordecai because his name is written in Aramaic under the belly of his horse. (Ahasuerus and Esther are likewise identified by inscriptions.) The background of the moment recorded in the painting is this: Mordecai had discovered and exposed a plot against the king's life. Sometime afterward the king learns by accident of Mordecai's good deed and that Mordecai has never been rewarded. The king inquires of Haman what he should do for a man he wishes to honor. Haman, thinking the king has him in mind, replies that the king should have such a man dressed in the king's royal robes, crowned with a royal crown on his head, placed on the king's horse, and led through the city by one of the king's most noble princes who shall proclaim, "Thus shall it be done to the man whom the king wishes to honor." In response to Haman's suggestion, the king tells Haman to do just what he had suggested—but for Mordecai not for Haman. Haman is to be the noble prince who is to lead Mordecai through the city, proclaiming, "Thus shall it be done to the man whom the king wishes to honor."[5] The scene in the Dura-Europos synagogue shows Mordecai being led through the city by the humiliated Haman.

In the painting, Mordecai is dressed in the full royal apparel of a Sassanian king: blue caftan, Iranian trousers, and a red coat with gold bands flowing out behind him. On his feet he wears soft white boots. It is the same costume that the king himself wears in the scene to the right. Strangely enough, neither Mordecai, nor the king appears to wear the golden crown referred to in Scripture. Instead, Mordecai wears a red cap; however, underneath the cap, indicated by a white line, is a royal diadem, the ends of which extend about his shoulders in a zigzag line. Beside Mordecai hangs a quiver of arrows.

Haman is pictured in degradation. His feet are bare, as is his head. As Goodenough points out, "He wears only a belted caftan whose short skirt barely covers his genitals."[6] He leads the horse like a slave groom.

The scene on the right is dominated by Ahasuerus. According to a tradition preserved in the *Targum* of Esther, a rabbinical paraphrase of the biblical book, Ahasuerus sat on the same throne once used by King Solomon. It is evident that the Dura-Europos artist was familiar with this legend, for, like the golden throne of King Solomon described in I Kings, Ahasuerus' golden throne at Dura-Europos is also approached by steps;

Dura-Europos—The western wall of the synagogue, which is fortunately the best preserved. The Torah shrine is in the center of the wall. To the right is a 5-stepped seat of honor. Directly above the Torah shrine is an obscure overpainted picture which has been the subject of endless scholarly debate, with an uncertain outcome. The synagogue's four portraits are on either side of the pictures above the Torah shrine. The "Esther" panel is immediately to the left of the Torah shrine. To the right of the Torah shrine is the prophet Samuel anointing Saul as Israel's first king. Further to the right, Moses is being rescued from the Nile.

89

above

Dura-Europos—The Esther panel. On the left, a humiliated Haman leads a regally dressed Moredecai through the streets of Shushan. In the center are four mysterious Greek-robed characters with a total of seven feet. On the right, Ahasuerus sits on Solomon's golden throne. Beside him is Queen Esther in a three-turreted golden diadem known as a Jerusalem of gold. This panel is discussed at length in the text.

left

Dura-Europos—Part of the panel depicting Moses' infancy. Pharoah's daughter stands naked in the Nile, having just removed the infant Moses from the gabled box. Above her stand three women apparently bearing gifts for the young boy who will save his people. On the left, the child has been handed to his Hebrew mother and sister.

Dura-Europos—Three of the four portraits from the synagogue. Each has a square halo and each is dressed in a Greek gown. The figure on the right is clearly Moses at the burning bush. The hand of God protrudes from heaven. The other two portraits may also be Moses, although there is no scholarly agreement on this. In the upper right, Moses—or is it Ezra?—reads the law. The figure on the left has a strange incomplete shadow which has no relation to the sun or moon above.

Dura-Europos—Detail of the Esther panel. Ahasuerus sits on Solomon's golden throne with Esther beside him wearing a golden, turreted crown. The golden throne differs in one detail from the description of Solomon's throne in 1 Kings. Instead of lions confronting each other on each of the steps, the lions alternate with eagles, as described in *Targum Sheni* of Esther, indicating that the Jews of Dura-Europos had absorbed the same traditional rabbinic materials which permeated normative Judaism.

opposite
Dura-Europos—The Torah shrine. A step leads up to the aedicula. A shell decorates the roof of the niche. Above the niche is a painting of a two-doored ark, also surmounted with a shell. On the left is a *lulav* and *etrog,* and a three-footed *menorah.* On the right is an unusual portrayal of the binding of Isaac. The figures all have their backs to us. Their heads are represented by black blobs. At the bottom is the ram under a tree, waiting to be substituted for Isaac. Above the ram is Abraham in a white robe; only his buttock is outlined. He holds an upraised knife. To the left is the child Isaac on the altar. At the top is another figure, back turned to us, inside a tent. Is this Sarah waiting below, Abraham's servant, or another picture of Abraham himself? And what does it mean? To the left of the tent is the hand of God telling Abraham to lay not his hand on his son.

and on either side of the throne itself is a crouching lion, just as King Solomon's throne is described in the Bible.

In one detail the throne of Ahasuerus at Dura-Europos differs from the throne of King Solomon described in I Kings 10:19-20. The biblical throne has lions confronting each other on the ends of each of the steps leading up to it. On the Dura-Europos throne of King Ahasuerus, the animals on the ends of the steps are, alternately, lions and eagles. This detail of Ahasuerus' throne is taken from one of the *Targumim* of Esther which also has the alternating lion and eagle motif. Thus, the Jews of Dura-Europos were familiar not only with details of the Bible but also with the traditional rabbinic *aggada,* a fact which will have considerable significance when we later ask ourselves whether Jews who worshipped in Dura-Europos and other synagogues with Hellenistic and oriental influences were traditional, normative Jews (see Chapter XI). The instance we have cited here is only one of several in which deviations from or additions to the biblical text in Dura-Europos art are based on the rabbinical *aggada* and in which the painter shows the influence of *Targum* and *Midrash.*[7]

Ahasuerus' Persian costume is similar to what we have seen on Mordecai. The king holds his legs in the peculiar position in which Sassanian kings are often represented. Queen Esther sits beside the king. She wears a tight blue bodice, with a long pink skirt and a drape wrapped around her legs. Adorned with necklace, earrings and bracelets, she alone wears a crown. Although scripture tells us she wore a crown (Esther 2:17), the one in the panel is an unusual one which has puzzled scholars. Recent studies have suggested that this golden crown, depicting three turrets as part of a city wall, was known in contemporary Jewish sources. This type of mural crown was referred to by the expression "City of Gold" or "Jerusalem of Gold." So the crown which Queen Esther wears may well be a depiction of the walls of Jerusalem.[8]

A long white veil falls from her head to her waist. She is of queenly bearing and propriety. Interestingly enough, the queen sits higher than the king. Under hieratic oriental influence, this is a clear indication of the paramount importance of Queen Esther, despite the fact that, as a woman, she is depicted as far smaller in size than the king. Behind the queen stands a figure who is probably Esther's personal maid. Beside and behind the king stand two men in Persian costume, who are probably his throne guards.

Another young man in Persian dress is holding up a scroll which he is either giving to the king or receiving from him. He is a messenger of some importance, wearing, as he does, a jeweled armband. Perhaps he holds the decree which the king's secretaries recorded, allowing the Jews to defend themselves and slay their enemies (Esther 8:8-14). Or perhaps it is a report of the Jews' enemies slain in Susa (Esther 9:11).

Finally, we are brought to the most puzzling part of the picture, the four men in the center of the panel. They are in a central position, but we have no idea who they are. They are dressed in typical Greek dress, consisting of a long gown with sleeves, known as a *chiton*, and a long rectangular shawl, known as a *himation*, which, as here, is ordinarily draped over the left shoulder, wound around the body just above the right hip, and held by throwing both ends over the left arm, thus leaving the right hand free. This Greek costume and the Persian costume already described are repeated frequently in the synagogue panels of Dura-Europos, but their combination here in one panel makes this one of the most striking examples of the mingling of Hellenistic and oriental influence—set in a purely Jewish context.

Are these men in Greek dress part of the crowd watching Mordecai led through the streets, as one scholar suggests? Or do they have some mysterious symbolic significance, as another suggests? They occupy such a prominent position in the panel that it is hard to imagine they play no part in the story which is being told, yet modern scholarship has not learned enough about Judaism at Dura-Europos to tell us what it is. The artist has drawn a total of seven legs and feet for the four men. And only three of the four hold up their hands. Was this because of the dictates of space or does it have a symbolic meaning?

Like most of the paintings in the Dura-Europos synagogue, the background of the Esther panel is a monochrome, in this case, green. Thus, the picture is without setting and without any indication of depth or space. The effect is to make the figures loom large. Perhaps this adds to the essential forcefulness with which the figures present themselves.

With the exception of the messenger, all faces look directly out of the picture. Frontality was the order of the day. The eyes appear to be staring. Mordecai on his horse looks not in front of him, but at the viewer. Even the gesturing king looks not in the direction of his gesture, but out of the picture, directly at us. The figures are fundamentally linear in character, each person being carefully outlined, fully contained within a solid form, and with features sharply defined.

94

Dura-Europos—This careful drawing of the Moses infancy panel was made by Herbert Gute immediately after excavation. In the hands of the Egyptian princess, Moses has no facial features; his face is simply an empty oval. Only after he is handed to his Hebrew mother and sister on the left does he attain features.

All of these characteristics belong to the traditions of oriental art. Yet at the same time we see presaged here many of the characteristics of early Byzantine art, especially Christian art.[9] All this is mixed with strong Hellenistic influences in a strictly Jewish setting in which details reflect a familiarity not only with the biblical text, but with *midrashic* and *aggadic* glosses as well.

On the other side of the Torah shrine is a panel showing scenes from the early life of Moses. We shall look only at two of these scenes, which read from right to left.

Flowing through the bottom of the entire panel is the Nile River. On either side of the river are bulrushes. In the river floats the ark from which the baby has just been removed. The floating ark is not the basket covered with pitch as described in the Bible but a small Hellenistic casket with a gabled roof.

Pharaoh's daughter, who has been bathing, stands in the river holding the baby. The water comes just above the Egyptian princess's knees. Apart from some considerable jewelry, she stands naked—on the holiest wall of the synagogue. As one scholar has noted, the Egyptian princess is portrayed with the "same emphasis upon the pudendum" that is customarily found in female deities of the east.[10]

Behind the princess, standing on the shore, are her three maids. In their hands they carry fluted dishes, a box in the form of a small casket, and a juglet, in all of which some commentators have found symbolic significance. Could the articles which the three maids hold be gifts to the newborn baby whose future will be of such significance for mankind—in the same oriental tradition in which gifts were brought to the infant Jesus?

In the scene to the left, Jochebed and Miriam, the mother and sister of Moses, hold the infant. Apparently Moses has just been passed to them, after Miriam's offer to find a Hebrew woman to suckle the child has been accepted by Pharaoh's daughter.

An intriguing touch in this panel is that the face of Moses is blank—without any features at all—in the hands of the Egyptian princess. (This appears more clearly in a copy of the painting made with painstaking care *in situ* by H. Gute the year after it was first excavated than in the original picture which is now in the Damascus Museum and which has been re-touched.) In the Gute painting, the face of the baby held by Pharoah's daughter has neither eyes, nose, nor mouth. Only when the baby is held by his Jewish mother and sister does he acquire features.

Above the Torah receptacle of the Dura-Europos synagogue are two large paintings which are flanked by four full length portraits, the only portraits in the synagogue. In all probability, all four of these portraits are of Moses, although others such as Abraham, Jacob, Enoch, Samuel, Joshua and Ezra have also been suggested. Of one portrait, there is no doubt as to its identity. Moses dressed in the Greek *chiton* and *himation* stands beside the burning bush. The plant is the same as the one the artist previously used to depict the bulrushes on the banks of the Nile, but this time it is larger. The red wavy lines are intended to depict the fire that burns without consuming the plant. Moses is barefoot, with his high boots beside him. A square protusion of the background sets off his head. It has been suggested that this is in fact a square halo. Above Moses' right shoulder is an inscription in Aramaic, "Moses, son of Levi". It is the only one of the four portraits so identified—in a picture that is unmistakably Moses. The hand of God extends from the vault of heaven above the burning brush.

The portrait below this one is perhaps the most moving face in the synagogue—composed, wise and mystical. The figure is again robed with the Greek *chiton* and *himation* and his head is again set off by a square halo. Instead of high boots, he wears sandals. In his hands he holds a scroll from which he reads the law (although his gaze is directed out of the picture, at the viewer, and although the wavy lines indicating the script appear on the wrong side of the scroll.) Ezra reading the law immediately comes to mind. But the fact that one of the other portraits in addition to the burning bush scene can almost certainly be identified as Moses suggests that this portrait too may be Moses. The difficulty is that we would not expect to see Moses reading from a scroll; we would expect him reading from tablets. However, it is possible that this is simply another anachronism—no more jarring than seeing Moses in Greek dress. Beside the figure stands an object draped with a red cloth. Its shape suggests a case for the Torah scroll, similar to the shape of the Torah cases still used by Sephardic communities.

Moses is also portrayed in a panel showing the crossing of the Red Sea and the drowning of the Egyptians. We shall not examine this panel in detail except to point out that it depicts Moses as a giant, holding what seems to be the club of Hercules, and leading the children of Israel across the Red Sea. Perhaps the Dura-Europos artist was trying to tell his congregants that Moses was as strong and powerful as the pagan Hercules.

7 ✡ BROADHOUSE-PLAN SYNAGOGUES

All over the ancient world—from North Africa to the Euphrates and in Israel too.

Having described the basilica-plan synagogue of Capernaum in detail, little more needed to be said about other basilica-plan synagogues for it was representative of its type. We devoted the last chapter to the broadhouse-plan synagogue at Dura-Europos for another reason: it is startlingly unique. However, to a large extent, almost every broadhouse-plan synagogue is unique. Just about the only characteristic shared by the broadhouse-plan synagogues is their basic shape—they are broader than they are long. That is, the synagogue room in broadhouse synagogues is oriented so that the long wall is the "front" wall. However, in most other respects, they are unlike one another. If unity is the primary characteristic of basilica-plan synagogues, diversity is the essential quality of broadhouse-plan synagogues.

There are far fewer broadhouse-plan synagogues than basilica-plan synagogues, so we might expect less rather than more diversity in these broadhouse-plans. However, the opposite is the case.

The basilica-plan synagogues were concentrated in the Galilee. Broadhouse-plan synagogues, on the other hand, have been found in many regions. Two broadhouse-plan synagogues have long been known south of Hebron in the Judean hills—Eshtamoa and Sussiya. Because of these two broadhouses in the southern part of Israel, scholars had thought of broadhouse-plan synagogues as characteristic of southern Palestine, just as basilica-plan synagogues were typical of northern Palestine. Then in 1968, three young American scholars began excavating a little known site, called Shema (with the accent on the first syllable), which, to everyone's surprise, turned out to contain a broadhouse-plan synagogue—in the heart of the area of basilica-plans.

We have already visited in these pages a broadhouse-plan as far east as the Euphrates River: Dura-Europos. Broadhouse-plans have also been found as far west as Tunisia, North Africa where archaeologists un-

Sussiya—A plan of this broadhouse synagogue. The prayer room is on the left. On the right is a large columned forecourt.

Synagogue

Forecourt

covered a beautiful broadhouse-plan synagogue at Hammam Lif and another at Priene in Asia Minor, just north of Miletus.

The architecture of the broadhouse-plans varies more than the architecture of the basilica-plans. The interior of the basilica-plans were all divided by rows of columns into naves and aisles; with a single exception, the basilica-plans were all entered by three doors in one of the short walls. Even this kind of consistency is absent in broadhouse-plans. Dura-Euro-

Sussiya—a synagogue inscription in Hebrew. The design—a rectangle with a small triangle on either side pointing toward the inscription—is typical. So are the contents of the inscription, which reads: "May the saintly master teacher Isi the priest (Cohan) be remembered for good. The honored eminent scholar made this mosaic and covered its walls with plaster, as he vowed at the feast of Rabbi Yochanan, the eminent priestly scribe, his son. Peace upon Israel. Amen."

opposite

Sussiya—This mosaic features a frequent motif in synagogue mosaics—a Torah ark with a three-footed *menorah* on either side. The *menorot* are not identical. Enough remains of the *menorah* on the right to confirm that the design included the usual *shofar* and *lulav*. The Torah ark consists of the typical panelled doors, mounted by a triangular pediment inside of which is a stylized shell. To the left of this motif stands a ram. Along the bottom is a swastika design.

Hammam Lif—The mosaic from this North African synagogue features lovely geometric designs, as well as birds and animals. Within the diamonds of the geometric design at left are various animals, birds, and baskets of fruit. In the upper center panel is a sea with fishes and ducks. In the lower center panel are date palms, a fountain, peacocks and other birds, set in a paradise scene. Between the upper and lower panels is a Latin inscription. The right panel includes a lion.

pos was, as we have seen, without interior columns in the synagogue room itself (although there were columns in a forecourt). Similarly the broadhouse-plan synagogue at Priene was without interior columns. But at Hammam Lif in North Africa and Shema in Galilee we find broadhouse-plan synagogues divided by two rows of columns. At Dura-Europos, the synagogue is entered by two doors in the long wall opposite the Torah shrine—a large door in the center supposedly for men and a small door at the end of the same wall for women. A similar arrangement was found at Priene. At Eshtamoa, on the other hand, the synagogue was entered from three doors on one of the short sides at a right angle to the Torah shrine, while at Hammam Lif the three entrances were placed on the long wall opposite the Torah shrine. At Shema, the main entrance, with a *menorah* on the lintel, was on the long wall, and a secondary entrance, with steps leading down into the synagogue was on the short wall.

Another variation within the broadhouse-plan synagogues appears to be in the provision they make for women worshippers, assuming, that is, that the women were segregated. (See page 63 for a discussion of this question). While some broadhouse-plans, such as Dura-Europos and Priene, probably had a one-floor plan with a separate section for women, other broadhouse-plans, as at Sussiya, had two floors with the second story possibly serving as a women's gallery.

Perhaps more dramatic are the contrast and variation in decoration of the two types of synagogues. The basilica-plan synagogues were heavily decorated on the outside, less heavily on the inside, in carved stone relief. In the broadhouse-plans, it is just the reverse. They are heavily decorated on the inside with almost no decoration on the outside. At Dura-Europos, this decoration consisted of magnificent biblical paintings. At Eshtamoa

some carved fragments reminiscent of basilica-plan ornamentation have been found. In broadhouse-plan synagogues, we also see mosaic floors for the first time in synagogue art.

The pattern of decoration is not as consistent in broadhouse-plans as in the basilica-plans. For example, the synagogue mosaic at Eshtamoa is limited to vegetable and geometric patterns (at least in the small part of the mosaic that has been preserved). At nearby Sussiya we find a mosaic of Daniel in the lion's den, reminiscent of the biblical paintings from Dura-Europos, and the wheel of a zodiac. Interestingly enough, this zodiac wheel was apparently changed into a purely geometric design. Conceptually half way between the Eshtamoa mosaic (which had no animal or human figures in its mosaic) and the Sussiya mosaic (which has not only a biblical scene but a pagan zodiac) is the beautiful mosaic of Hammam Lif, which emphasizes lovely geometric designs together with birds and animals in a paradise scene.

Many of the abundant synagogue inscriptions, not only in broadhouse-plans, but in other plans as well, are in Greek and Aramaic. Curiously enough among the rarer Hebrew inscriptions, we find several at Sussiya. Thus the unusual Hebrew inscription, in the Holy Tongue rather than in Greek or Aramaic, is in a synagogue with a representational mosaic (Daniel in the lion's den)—in contravention of the Second Commandment?—and a pagan zodiac. It seems impossible to impose patterns on broadhouse-plan synagogues.

Until very recently many scholars characterized the broadhouse-plan

Shema—Recently excavated and restored, this synagogue had two entrances. The main entrance was at the right. The lintel—not yet restored to its place above the entrance—contained a *menorah*. The secondary entrance was by the steps in the upper part of the picture. The *bema* extends from the far long wall into the synagogue. A color picture of this synagogue appears on the dust jacket.

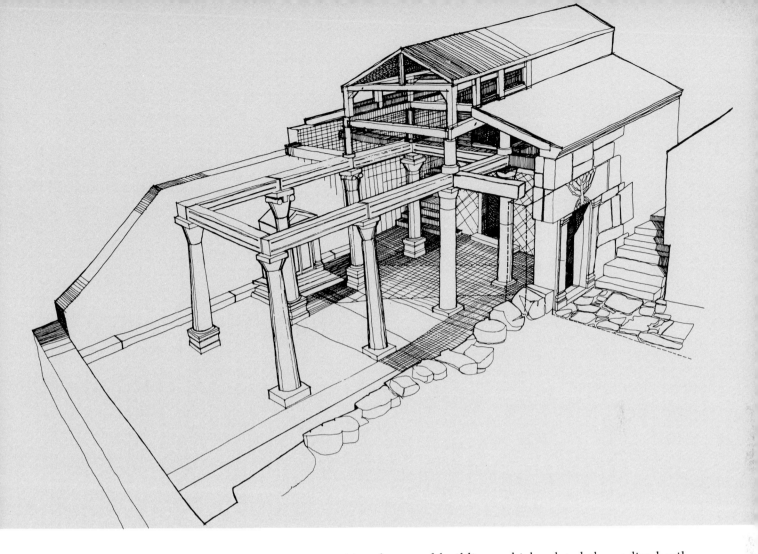

Shema—A reconstruction of the synagogue, showing the entrance with the *menorah* lintel, a Torah ark on the far wall, the steps of the second entrance, and clerestory windows in the roof to let in the light.

Shema—A *menorah* appears on this lintel which was originally part of the main entrance to the synagogue. It is the largest *menorah* ever recovered from an ancient site.

synagogue as a transitional type of building, which related the earlier basilica-plans to the later apse-plans. Here, in the broadhouse-plans, the synagogue architects were trying to create an appropriate design for a synagogue with a permanent receptacle for the Scroll of the Law; they were experimenting with new ideas. The argument concluded that out of all this eventually emerged the apse-plan in the fifth or sixth century.[1]

However, even the principal proponent of this position, Professor

Michael Avi-Yonah of The Hebrew University, has recently shifted ground. Although he retains the term "transitional" to describe these broadhouse-plan synagogues, he now concedes that "the bewildering variety of plans among [this type] precludes any attempt to use them as a basis to determine chronology."[2] Yet if these synagogue plans have no chronological relation to buildings before or after, it is difficult to see how they can be characterized as transitional. One suspects that in time this term will be dropped.

The second broadhouse-plan synagogue at Dura-Europos is dated to 245 C.E. But the excavators found evidence of a synagogue there which was probably built on the same site 50 or 75 years earlier. It too was a broadhouse-plan. So here we have a late second century broadhouse-plan built at about the same date as the earliest Galilean basilica-plans. The first synagogue at Shema, another broadhouse, is dated to the third century, which is especially surprising to find in the Galilee—the heart of the basilica-plan area—and contemporaneous with these basilica-plans. Other broadhouse-plans extend through time and were built and used simultaneously with the generally later apse-plan synagogues.

As we shall see in more detail when we discuss apse-plan synagogues, there is an obvious relationship between the basilica-plan synagogues and the later apse-plan synagogues. The latter basically adds an apse to the earlier basilica-plan for use as a permanent Torah shrine. But the broadhouse-plan does not appear to fit onto this pattern. Indeed, it is not an essentially Graeco-Roman building. It may have developed from a private house or possibly even from the architecture of oriental pagan temples.[3] Other broadhouse-plans may have developed from the requirements of the site or the desire to use already existing walls or even as a result of architectural creativity.[4] Thus, there is great doubt as to whether the broadhouse-plan synagogues deserve a separate category, for the only uniting factor

Eshtamoa—The remains of the Torah shrine in the northern wall, facing Jerusalem. In the lower left are the remains of a platform (bema) which extended into the prayer hall. Above are three niches built into the wall, a larger center niche where the Torah was kept and smaller niches on either side which probably held menorot. Wooden steps led up to the niches, which are six feet above the floor. Notice the stepped benches to the right of the platform, honored seats on the Jerusalem wall.

Eshtamoa—A mosaic of solely geometric designs includes a large center rosette. No possibility here of a violation of the Second Commandment's prohibition of images. At the bottom of the picture, below the squared stones, are the remains of an earlier mosaic. Included in the designs of this earlier mosaic (the lowest row in the picture) is a form of a swastika, a common design in antiquity.

among their small number is that they are broader than they are long, with the Torah shrine located on the long side.

Moreover, it is difficult to see how the broadhouse-plan synagogues are related to the development of a Torah shrine. The synagogue at Dura-Europos indicates that the structural Torah shrine was known when the earliest basilica-plan synagogues were built.[5] Apparently the use of a permanent Torah shrine was a development that occurred over a period of perhaps 150 or 200 years or more. During much of this period a portable Torah shrine was still optional though its use gradually dwindled. But even at a very early time some synagogues already had a structural niche for the Scroll of the Law.

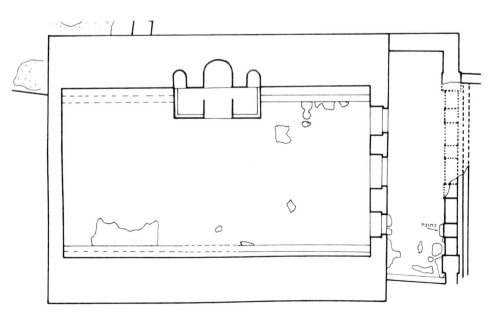

Eshtamoa—a plan of the synagogue. Note the entrances on the short wall. In the medieval period, the building was converted to a mosque.

As a group, the broadhouse-plans illustrate some of the imaginative variety with which Torah shrines were created. We have already seen the Torah shrine at Dura-Europos. By contrast, consider the lovely three-niched Torah shrine of Eshtamoa with its large central niche for the Torah and two smaller niches on either side which the excavators suggest were used for *menorot*, all of which was approached by now destroyed steps. (Incidentally, that the two smaller niches were in fact used for *menorot* is suggested by a number of synagogue mosaics, in which the Torah ark is shown flanked on both sides by *menorot*.)

There were other variations in broadhouse-plan synagogues. Some had *bemot*, stands for reading the Law, adjacent to the Torah shrine. One of the broadhouse-plan synagogues, Shema, was entered by descending steps, rather than ascending, so that the synagogue room itself gives a feeling of being sunken, perhaps in compliance literally with the dramatic opening verse of Psalm 130:

Out of the depths I call to thee, O Lord.

Thus, as a group, the broadhouse-plan synagogues are important not so much for their relationships, either to one another or to other synagogue plans, but precisely for the opposite reason. They have no relationship. They are independent. It is as if they were intended to proclaim that ancient synagogues will not be confined to scholar's categories. The broadhouse-plan synagogues, several of them fully excavated only within the last four or five years, indicate that ancient synagogues were far richer and more varied than almost anyone supposed. Perhaps the future, rather than enabling us better to categorize these synagogues, will only add to their variety.

Shema—Workers reconstructing the excavated remains.

8 ✡ APSE-PLAN SYNAGOGUES

Of mosaics and Torah shrines

The third and final type of synagogue plan we shall look at is what I have called the apse plan: It is a basilica plan with a bubble at the end.* The apse represents the final stage in the development of the Torah shrine, which, as we have seen, has been at the center of the development of synagogue architecture.

There was no structural Torah shrine in the earliest stages of the basilica-plan synagogues in and around Galilee. The Ark of the Law was mobile; it was brought in for the Torah reading during the service and then removed. The next stage involved the conversion of some of these synagogues to provide a permanent installation (or *adyton*) for the Torah ark in front of the main entrance to the synagogues. This blocked the main entrance to the synagogue; the two smaller entrances on either side of the main entrance were then used by the congregation for ingress and egress. In other synagogues, a structural niche or *aedicula* was created in the wall facing Jerusalem, and in this the Torah was placed. A niche like this could be made by blocking up an entrance and leaving an indentation, instead of making the inside of the blocked entrance flush with the wall. (This was done, as we shall see, at the Ein-Gedi synagogue). In new synagogues the niche could be designed as part of the original structure. (This was the case with the *aedicula* at Dura-Europos and other broadhouse-plan synagogues, but it was also done in at least one Galilean basilica-plan synagogue, at Arbel.) It is not entirely clear whether these Torah niches were permanent housings for the Torah and ark, or the Torah was placed

*In fact what I have called basilica-plans and apse-plans are both varieties of Graeco-Roman basilicas, one with and the other without an apse. Both forms were prevalent in Graeco-Roman architecture at a very early period. My terminology has been chosen simply to distinguish between the two types, not to suggest that apse-plans are not basilicas.

there during the service when it was not being read.[1] Finally, synagogues were designed with an apse, which was for the express purpose of permanently housing the Ark of the Law containing the Torah scrolls. The apse was usually approached by several steps and was separated from the congregation either by a screen—the fragments of several such apse screens have survived—or, later, by a curtain (as we shall see it pictured in mosaics).

It would be a mistake to view this development of the Torah shrine as linear. It is true that the earliest synagogues had no place for a permanent Torah shrine or even a niche where the Torah could be placed during the service. It is also true that the apse was a later development for the housing of the Ark of the Law. But in between there was a great deal of overlap. There were some very early Torah shrines, but other later synagogues (Ostia and Sardis) were built without Torah shrines and were used in this way long after structural Torah shrines became the general rule.[2]

The Ark of the Law as a permanent feature of synagogue architecture was opposed by some elements of the community. In certain conservative circles the ark was seen as a kind of substitute for or imitation of the sanctuary in the destroyed Temple. To these people, the Ark of the Law in the synagogue was a desecration. They referred to the Ark of the Law as an *arona* (coffin) rather than *aron ha-kodesh* (ark or chest of holiness).[3] However, their view did not prevail.

In the standard apse-plan synagogue, the apse was oriented toward Jerusalem and the congregants entered the synagogue from three doors on the opposite wall. Thus they faced the Holy Ark and Jerusalem as they entered; they did not have to turn around as was required on entering the early synagogues without Torah shrines whose front facades were oriented toward Jerusalem. The apse was semi-circular, although in some cases, as at Priene, Jerash and the earlier synagogue at Hammath-Gader, it was square or rectangular.

Instead of the three rows of columns which we saw in the basilica-plan synagogues, apse-plan synagogues usually had only two rows of columns forming two side aisles and a central nave.[4] Outside we often find a narthex or entrance hall.

Apse-plan synagogues appear to have been built as early as the end of the fourth century and continued to be built until about the end of the seventh or beginning of the eighth century. Within that period of more than 300 years, it is difficult, if not impossible, to date apse-plan synagogues on the basis of architectural evidence. Occasionally an inscription may help us. In recent excavations, more refined archaeological methods provide other clues to dating. But for most apse-plans, there is no reliable date within this period. Often we are left with a wide variety of what can only be described as scholarly guesses. For example, various scholars date the apse-plan synagogue at Jericho to the fourth, sixth or seventh, and eighth centuries.[5] All that can be said with confidence is that the apse-plan is the prevailing synagogue plan during the centuries following the basilica-plan synagogues.

But in a way, this is an important datum because it explains one of the most significant differences between basilica-plan synagogues and apse-plan synagogues: their manner of decoration. It is the difference between the Age of Rome and the Byzantine Age. Reflected in synagogue architecture, this meant that the impressive exterior decoration of the Hellenistic-Roman basilica-plans with their elaborate high relief carving gave way to stark external simplicity. The urge to decoration was transferred instead

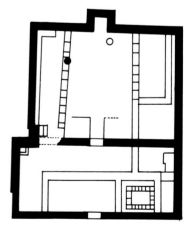

Priene—This plan of the excavation shows the synagogue, with its square apse, in solid black.

to the interior in apse-plan synagogues, and it was here that the synagogue architect now released his creative energy. This change is attributable to general stylistic differences between the Byzantine Age and the age that preceded it as well as the peculiar situation of the Jews within the larger culture. The end of the second century and the beginning of the third century, to which we assign the basilica-plan synagogues, was one of Roman tolerance, even friendship, for Jews. This was followed a hundred years later by the Age of Constantine who in 325 converted to Christianity and ushered in the Byzantine period. Christianity became the state religion of the Roman Empire, and, to put it bluntly, this was not good for the Jews. Within less than a hundred years of Constantine's conversion to Christianity, Jews were forbidden by law to construct new synagogues or to repair old ones unless they threatened to collapse.[6] This law was not scrupulously observed, which might well have been the result of efficient bribery. But an elaborate display of Jewish public buildings was not the order of the day in Byzantine times and Jews were well-advised to confine the decoration of their new houses of worship to the interior.

Extant synagogue ruins indicate that this interior decoration consists

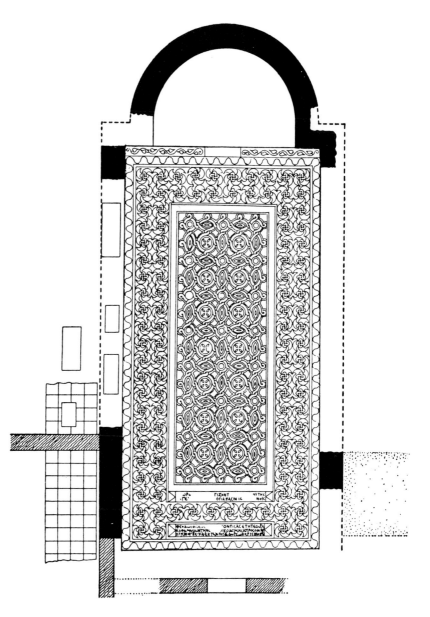

Aegina—This synagogue mosaic contains no representations whatever, only geometric designs, including swastikas with rounded arms.

107

principally of mosaic floors which appear to have been the pavement of almost every apse-plan synagogue, replacing the plain flagstones used in basilica-plan synagogues. (We can only guess what the walls were like. Could they have contained pictures like the Dura-Europos synagogue, whose walls were saved by a quirk of fate?)

Since it is difficult to find any meaningful linear development in these mosaic floors—we have already seen how difficult they are to date—we can only record their truly bewildering variety, each with its own peculiar authentic appeal. These mosaic pavements also reflect diverse attitudes toward what is permitted in synagogue decoration—and it is in terms of these attitudes that we have organized our presentation.

One of the most conservative of synagogue mosaics is the beautiful carpet in the synagogue of Aegina, that jewel of a Greek isle set in the Aegean Sea. The design covers every square centimeter of the floor. Over and over again, we shall see this Byzantine compulsion to fill every bit of space—scholars call the compulsion *horror vacui*. The design at Aegina is wholly geometric. It resembles a carpet. The border design consists principally of swastikas with rounded arms. In the center of the carpet is another geometric design. Not even a ritual object such as a *menorah* is depicted. It would be difficult to know that the building was a synagogue were it not for a Greek inscription which mentions an *archisynagogus*.[8]

We shall not speak much of the building at Aegina. As with most apse-plan synagogues, very little of it is left. Usually we find mere stubs of walls, often barely sufficient to trace the outline of the building. We may be able to discern the line of the walls and the outline of the apse, perhaps with the steps leading up to it, but little more. The ravages of time and the need of neighbors for stones to build with have taken care of the rest. Therefore, we shall focus on the surviving mosaic.

The Jericho synagogue, located less than a kilometer from the tell of ancient Jericho, is, like the Aegina synagogue, geometric, but the Jericho mosaic also includes representations of certain synagogue appurtenances and ritual objects. Near the center of the floor is a circle containing the most popular and ubiquitous Jewish symbol in synagogue art, especially from the fourth century on: the seven-branched candelabra or *menorah*. On the left is a *lulav* or palm branch used in the celebration of *Sukkot*, and on the right is a *shofar* or ram's horn which is still blown in the synagogue on the High Holy Days—*Rosh Hashanah* and *Yom Kippur*. This combination of symbols is repeated over and over again in synagogue art.

It may come as a surprise to modern readers to learn that the frequent appearance of the *menorah* in synagogue art raises a serious problem of religious law. Three different passages in the Talmud forbid the making of a *menorah* similar to the one in the Temple, regardless of the material used.[9] Just as some Jews objected to the use of an Ark of the Law—calling it, with the use of a Hebrew pun, a coffin[10]—in the belief that any effort to re-create an image of the destroyed Temple was a desecration of its memory, some Jews opposed the reproduction of the Temple *menorah*. Perhaps the rabbinic prohibition against reproduction of the seven-branched Temple *menorah* was early interpreted as a prohibition against the making of a three dimensional *menorah* which could actually be used as a candelabrum[11], rather than against the representation of two-dimensional *menorot* in mosaics, paintings and reliefs; however, some scholars suggest that the original prohibition was broader,[12] and we do find two-dimensional *menorot* of five, six and nine branches, apparently to avoid this

A five-branched *menorah* from a mosaic in a private home in Beth Shean. The Talmud states that, "A man may not make . . . a *menorah* similar to the sacred *menorah*, but he may make one with five or six or eight lamps, but with seven he should not make." (Babylonian Talmud, Rosh Hashanah).

overleaf top left (text, see p. 122).
Beth Alpha—The zodiac from the center panel of the mosaic floor. In the corners are the four seasons. The twelve signs of the zodiac are depicted around the wheel. Both the seasons and the signs are identified in Hebrew. In the center is the Greek god Helios in his four-horsed chariot putting the night to flight. The mosaicist had only modest ability, but his work has a charming, unsophisticated, folk-art quality.

overleaf bottom left
Beth Alpha—The binding of Isaac. On the right is the altar with its flames leaping up. Abraham, holding a knife, is about to place the boy on the altar. Both Abraham and Isaac are identified in Hebrew. From heaven the hand of God protrudes: "Lay not . . ." says the Hebrew inscription, quoting the Bible. The ram is shown caught in the thicket. At the bottom of the mountain, Abraham's two servants wait with the donkey.

overleaf top right
Beth Alpha—The center of the zodiac depicting Helios with seven shafts of sunlight emanating from his head. He rides in a chariot with four galloping horses, each with a slightly different face. The day is near: Most of the stars have fallen to the bottom of the picture. There is great life in the horses and great strength in Helios' face.

overleaf bottom right
Beth Alpha—The Torah ark panel from the mosaic floor. A *ner tamid* or eternal light hangs from the apex of the ark. On either side of the ark is a lion, a three-footed *menorah*, a bird of uncertain identity and meaning, and a curtain. The curtain on the left side has been largely destroyed by a *bema* which was built over at a later stage.

proscription. (The illustration shows the remains of a five-branched *menorah* from the so-called House of Leontas at Beth Shean.) Moreover, even though the narrower interpretation of the talmudic restriction (limiting the prohibition to three-dimensional representations) would explain the appearance of the *menorah* in the Jericho synagogue mosaic and in other synagogue mosaics, this would not explain some three-dimensional *menorot*, which could be used, that have been found in excavations.

One usable seven-branched *menorah* was found in 1921 during excavations of a synagogue on the shores of the Sea of Galilee, known as Hammath Tiberias. The excavators found the top of an actual *menorah* made from a single block of stone, with seven branches cut in relief and a hollow receptacle for a wick on each branch. The *menorah*, now a part of the permanent collection of the Israel Museum in Jerusalem, retains the black burn marks that attests to its heavy use. To this *menorah* must now be added the top of a unique three-dimensional bronze *menorah* found in the excavation of a synagogue at Ein-Gedi in 1970 (see p. 134). These finds indicate that the seven-branched *menorah* was not only pictured in synagogue art, but was actually recreated in the round and used in the synagogue. This is further suggested by several mosaics—some of which we shall soon see—showing the Ark of the Law flanked on either side by a large *menorah*. These mosaics are presumably representations of the Ark of the Law in synagogues at the time. This kind of evidence led the excavators of the broadhouse-plan synagogue at Eshtamoa, with its lovely triple-niched Torah shrine, to reconstruct it with a Torah in the central niche and free-standing *menorot* in the smaller side niches. All of this suggests that even if the talmudic prohibition against making a *menorah* similar to the Temple *menorah* is interpreted as forbidding only three-dimensional *menorot* and not paintings or mosaics, we still have a problem: for three-dimensional *menorot* were apparently in common synagogue use at the very time these talmudic prohibitions were being formulated.

Perhaps these *menorot* were considered non-offending because they

Hammath Tiberias—A seven-branched *menorah* carved in limestone that bears the charred evidence of actual use.

above (text, p. 120)
Hammath Gader—Detail of a lion with upraised tail and exposed genitals.

right (text, p. 121)
Gaza—David—identified in Hebrew—playing a lyre and, like Orpheus, taming wild beasts with his music.

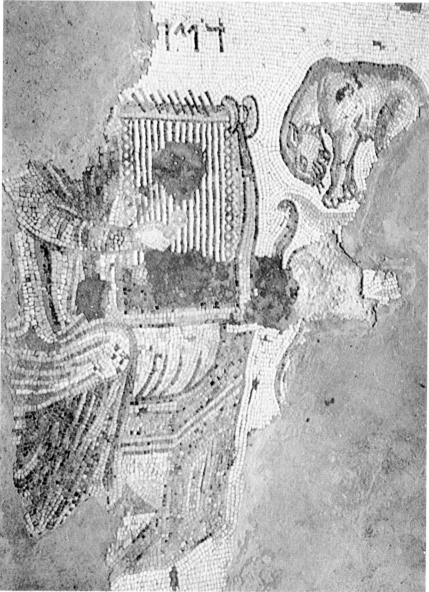

111

deviated in some detail or other from the *menorah* that was used in the Temple—the exact appearance of which is also a matter of scholarly debate[13]—or perhaps the intense desire of the people to depict and use the *menorah* as a Jewish symbol, reminiscent of the glories of their destroyed Temple, was too strong to be resisted by the formalistic objection of the rabbis whose views became enshrined in talmudic law. It would not be the first time that popular desire overrode rabbis' wishes.[14]

Let us return to the Jericho synagogue mosaic floor. Above the circle enclosing the *menorah* is a rectangular pattern superimposed on the background geometric design. To look at this rectangular design, one might conclude that it is nothing more than that—a pleasing design in the center of the floor. But upon closer examination it becomes apparent that it is a stylized representation of an Ark of the Law—a fact which is confirmed by the frequent use of the Ark of the Law in synagogue mosaics, as we shall see. In the Jericho ark, the two panelled doors are closed. They are surrounded by the frame of the ark, which is supported by four tiny legs. Above the ark, we usually find a triangular gable in the center of which is a shell. At Jericho, we see a stylized shell, but, strangely enough, the gable is missing.

The next mosaic we shall look at comes from an apse-plan synagogue at a site near the southern shore of the Sea of Galilee known as Hammath-Gader. In ancient times, Hammath-Gader was the Miami Beach of its day. Only a few miles from the Sea of Galilee, it abounds in hot springs of varying temperatures which were thought to provide a cure for a wide variety of diseases, from rheumatism to catarrh. Apparently, Jews who regularly visited Hammath-Gader contributed to the synagogue, as is indicated by the large number of inscriptions commemorating gifts from Jews of other cities which have been found here. Although inscriptions recording donations are common in ancient synagogues, regardless of the location or the plan of the synagogue, the number of these inscriptions is unusual at Hammath-Gader. Just in front of the steps leading up to the apse is a particularly lovely mosaic inscription, enclosed in a wreath with trailing ribbons. The wreath with its knot is recognizable as the one which was customarily awarded in the Hellenistic world to the victors in athletic and literary contests and to citizens who had distinguished themselves in the service of the state or as public benefactors. The Talmud itself reflects the

opposite
Hammath Tiberias—A mosaic floor similar to Beth Alpha, containing a zodiac and a Torah ark, but done with superb craftsmanship. The synagogue sits on the shore of the Sea of Galilee which may be seen in the background. A later synagogue wall was built over the mosaic.

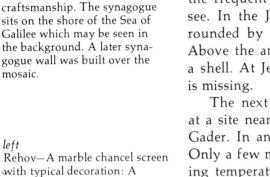

left
Rehov—A marble chancel screen with typical decoration: A *menorah* enclosed in a Hellenistic wreath tied in a Herculean knot.

right
Ashdod—A marble chancel screen which separated the apse from the rest of the synagogue. The decoration is typical: A three-footed *menorah* enclosed in a Hellenistic wreath with a Herculean knot. A *shofar* and *lulav* fill the space beside the menorah. A Greek inscription decorates the upper border of the screen.

Hammath-Gader—A closer view of the remains of the lion mosaic.

Hammath-Gader—A reconstruction of the mosaic carpet.

fact that Jews too conferred honors by wreaths in a form created by their Hellenistic neighbors.[15] The wreath in the synagogue floor was apparently intended to represent such an honor to the benefactor whose donation is commemorated thereby.

Most ancient synagogue inscriptions are in Greek and Aramaic. Occasionally, we find a few Hebrew words such as "*Shalom*" or "Peace unto Israel," but this is not as common. The inscription in the wreath at Hammath-Gader is in Aramaic, with Greek titles. It reads:

And remembered be for good Kyris (i.e. Mr.) Hoples, and Kyra (i.e. Madame) Protone, and Kyris Sallustius his son-in-law, and Comes (the honored) Phroros, his son, and Kyris Photios his son-in-law, and Kyris Haninah his son—they and their children—whose acts of charity are constant everywhere (and) who have given here

117

ΕΥΛΟΓΙΑ † ΗΟΘΛΑ

ΚΑΡΤΕΡΙΗΣΤΟΔΕΣΗΜΑ..ΨΑΝΟΝΦΕΡΕΙΦΟΙΤΟΝ
ΑΣΦΘΗΤΟΝΗΕΛΑΜΠΡΑΝ ωΖΟΗΜΝΙΑΝΓΕΝΑΙΗΣ
ΘΗΚΑΤΟΔΕΜΙΝΕΝΘΑΔΕΖΗΝΟΒΙΑ
ΜΗΤΕΡΟΣΕΗΣΤΙΟΥΣ. ΗΜΟΣΥΝΑΣ

ΤΟΥΤΟΣΟΙΜΑΚΑΡΤΑΤΗΚΑΡΠΟΣΟΕΔΙΜΑΤΟ
ΗΝΤ.ΚΕΣΕΖΑΓΑΠωΗΕΥΣΕΒΗΗΛΑΓΡΟΗωΝ
ΡΕΖΩΤΑΗΛΥΣΤΑΕΡΓΑΕΝΙΦΘΙΜΕΝΟΙΣΑΙΕΙ
ΟΦΡΑ.ΔΗΛΗΤ.ωΚΑΙΗΕΤΑΤΟ.ΡΜΑΒΙΟΥ
ΝΕΟΙ..ΔΑΣΚΥΛΕΥΤΟΝΑΥΘΙΣΕΧΟΤΕΠΛΟΥΤΟΝ

five denarii (of) gold. May the King of the Universe bestow the blessing upon their work. Amen. Amen. Selah.

The inscription is typical in asking that the donor and his family be remembered for good, that a blessing be bestowed upon them and in recording the fact of the gift. Another typical formula expresses the hope that the donor shall have a share in the world to come. The inscription in the Hammath-Gader synagogue is somewhat unusual in that it mentions the deity

Ashkelon—This marble plaque contains a three-footed *menorah*, with a *shofar* and incense shovel on the left and a *lulav* and *etrog* on the right. The inscription is in Greek.

Tiberias—An unusual synagogue chancel screen carved in a latticework diamond pattern with circles at the points of intersection. While the pattern is unusual in Jewish art, it is common in the Christian world of Byzantium. The menorah on the upper frame is flanked by stylized birds or ducks with partly mutilated heads. The size of the screen is typical, a little over two feet wide, and slightly less than two feet high.

right
Sussiya—A marble chancel post inscribed in Aramaic. The right picture shows the front of the top of the post. The left picture shows the side of the same post; at the bottom of the left picture can be seen the slot into which the chancel screen fits.

below
Sussiya—This inscription appears in the upper frame of the chancel screen which was supported by two chancel posts like that pictured right. It is a typical synagogue inscription, commemorating the names of the donors: "Remembered be for good Lazar and Isai, sons of Simeon, son of Lazar."

119

("the King of the Universe") and in the fact that it states the amount of the donation.[16] Scholars are not certain of the value of a gold denarius (it was equivalent to 24 silver denarii), but it must have been worth a great deal indeed for five of them to justify such long and central treatment in the synagogue's mosaic floor.[17]

On either side of the wreath enclosing the inscription is a lion. Although the mosaic itself is not in a good state of preservation, the lions themselves are beautifully alive, with heavy manes, tails gracefully held above their backs and red tongues protuding. Each detail of this portion of the mosaic had been meticulously laid—even to the deliberately exposed genitals.

Among the other finds at Hammath-Gader were scores of fragments of a carved apse screen which were scattered throughout the excavation area. Made of beautiful white marble, the apse screen originally separated the apse with its Ark of the Law from the remainder of the synagogue. From its fragments, it appears that the apse screen was deliberately and wantonly destroyed; despite the large number of fragments, it is beyond reconstruction. However, we can get a reasonably good idea of what it looked like from larger fragments found in other synagogues—at Ashkelon, Rehov, Ashdod, and Myndos in Asia Minor. A particularly lovely apse screen was recently published from Tiberias, on the southern end of the Sea of Galilee. Made of white marble almost 3 inches thick, the screen itself is 27 inches wide and 23 inches high. It is handsomely carved in a latticework diamond pattern with circles at the intersections. In the center of the top of the frame, a three-footed, seven-branched *menorah* is carved. The *menorah* is flanked by two birds or possibly ducks swimming in water.[18] In the course of recent excavations at the Sussiya synagogue, in Judah near Hebron, part of the ornamented frame of a chancel screen was uncovered which bore a typical synagogue inscription in Hebrew "Remembered be for good Lazar and Isai, sons of Simeon, son of Lazar."[19] As can be seen from the illustrations, apse screens consisted essentially of carved marble pillars to which a decorated marble screen was attached. Sometimes, as at Sussiya, the chancel posts were also inscribed—here, as is so frequently the case, to commemorate the donor.[20] Many scholars believe that these Jewish apse screens were the source of the Christian *iconostasis* or chancel screen, later adopted by the church.[21] One striking example of this influence of the synagogue on the church comes from a column of the synagogue apse screen at Myndos, which is duplicated almost exactly in the later chancel screen columns from two early churches at Jerash.[22]

Our next mosaic takes us south, within a few miles of Israel's pre-1967 border. Israel's policy of creating settlements as close to its borders as possible has not only been successful from a defense viewpoint, but occasionally it has also yielded archaeological dividends as well. In 1957 near a *kibbutz* settlement known as Nirim, south of Gaza, just outside the Gaza Strip, workers on a small side road came upon a synagogue mosaic which thrilled Israelis because it proved the presence of a Jewish community in the sixth century at a point considerably further south than had theretofore been uncovered. Jews, we now know, lived in ancient Ma'on.

This mosaic takes us considerably beyond the lions which we found at Hammath-Gader. After all, even Solomon's Temple had lions. But at ancient Ma'on we find a whole menagerie, a veritable zoo. The pattern of the Ma'on mosaic is created by grape vines growing out of an amphora, or wide-rimmed vase, at the lower end of the floor. The vines then form an endless series of circles, in each of which is some fruit or, more often, an animal. The craftsman paid attention to detail. We have no difficulty in recognizing a wide variety of animals: leopard, ibex, buffalo, sheep, rabbit, stag, elephant, peacock, partridge, flamingo, crane, dove, pheasant, guinea-fowl, hen, goose, and, of course, lion. A paw-footed *menorah* is at the top center, in the place of honor.[23]

Among the many interesting finds at Ma'on were also some glass handles and rims of goblets which the excavators tell us may well have belonged to the synagogue's *kiddush** or *havdalah*** cup.

A most curious thing about the Ma'on mosaic is its striking similarity to another mosaic found only a few miles away. This other mosaic, known as the Shellal mosaic, was discovered in 1917 by some Australian soldiers at the base of a Turkish trench after the Second Battle of Gaza. The Australians took the mosaic back with them to Australia and it is now the prize exhibit at the Canberra War Memorial.[24] The similarity between the Ma'on and Shellal mosaics is especially noteworthy because the former comes from a synagogue and the latter from a church. Here is another example of the close relationship between early synagogue and early church art. Quite possibly the same artist or the same workshop designed and executed both mosaics.

We now turn east of the Jordan to the site of Jerash, ancient Gerasa. There, as we have already mentioned in an earlier chapter, are the remains of a synagogue mosaic that depicts the biblical story of the Flood, complete with pairs of animals. Unfortunately, the ark and Noah, undoubtedly part of the design, did not survive. But, we can recognize the dove with a twig in its beak signifying the end of the flood and the remains of two human figures labelled in Greek "Shem" and "Japheth," two of Noah's three sons. Thus we have progressed from the geometric carpet at the Aegina synagogue to the portrayal of human figures from the Bible.

The discovery of a synagogue mosaic in the Gaza Strip shortly before the Six Day War provides the next step in our progression of synagogue mosaics. The Gaza synagogue too portrays a biblical figure—this time King David with his crown—but it does not have a biblical scene. Instead, we see King David as Orpheus, playing his lyre and taming wild beasts (see color illustration). It is as if the hellenized Jews who commissioned this mosaic were saying, "Our King David can do the same things your Orpheus can do." After all, David was a famous musician, as well as a composer of psalms. Shortly after the Six Day War, when Israeli scholars went to examine this Gaza mosaic, they found that the Egyptians had left it unprotected. The local citizenry had, doubtless from motives of vandalism rather than sectarian malice, destroyed the head of King David.

We end our brief survey of apse-plan synagogues by examining a synagogue with one of the best preserved and wildly extravagant mosaics ever to be found in an ancient synagogue. It is also one of the most difficult mosaics to interpret and understand.

The Beth Alpha synagogue is located in the Jezreel Valley not far from Beth Shean. No historic or literary memory is bound up with the site of

*The prayer at the beginning of the Sabbath meal which sanctifies the occasion. It is accompanied by the drinking of a cup of wine.
**The ceremony at the end of the Sabbath which marks the separation between the Sabbath and the rest of the week.

Beth Alpha. It is not in the center of anything; it was located in what can be described as a cultural hinterland. The community was distinguished by nothing more than the fact that a group of Jews decided to build a synagogue there.

The apse of the synagogue is oriented approximately south, in the direction of Jerusalem, as we have come to expect. The apse is on a raised platform and is approached by three steps. Beneath the apse was found a hoard of coins; apparently here was a *genizah* or depository for synagogue valuables. Benches line the walls, and a gallery above the main floor on three sides of the building might have served as the women's section. The gallery was reached by stairs in an adjoining room, rather than the outside

Ma'on—The synagogue mosaic from Nirim is almost identical to the church mosaic at Shellal, except for the Jewish symbols pictured here: Two lions facing a *menorah*, and a *shofar* beside the *menorah*. The palm trees below the lions are also a Jewish decoration.

Ma'on—Details of the mosaic

Basket with pomegranates

Ibex

Doves

Hare

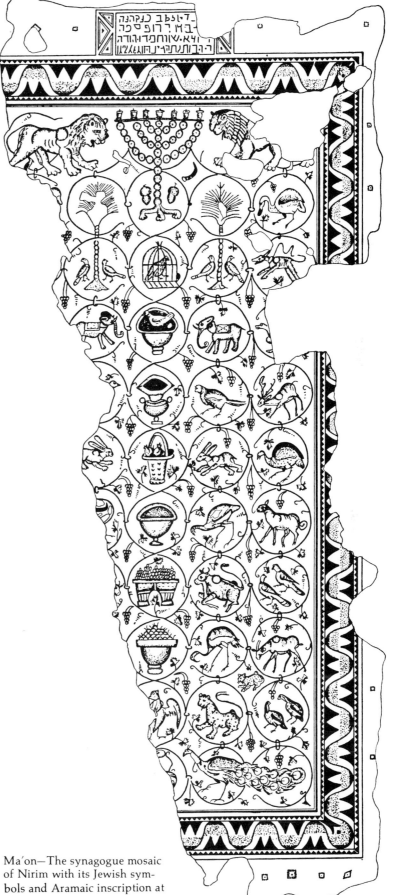

Ma'on—The synagogue mosaic of Nirim with its Jewish symbols and Aramaic inscription at top.

+ΤΟΝΔΕΤΟΝΝΕΘΝΛΛΑΤΙΛΕΙ
ΜΗC/ΝΟΤΕΘCΙΜΤΗΜΩΝΕ
ΚΑΙΘΕΘΦΙΛ. ΓΕΙ ΡΡΜΙΘΘΙ
ΝΛΡΙΘCΕΝΤΩΚΧΕΤΕΙΚΑΤ

ΥΜΕΜΑΡ
ΙΑΚΑΝ
ΙΔΑΙΟ
ΚΕΤΩΝ
ΛΛΩΔΕ
ΤΤΟΥ
ΜΟC
ΤΟΝΝΕ
ΘC

The Shellal church mosaic pictured here probably comes from the same workshop as the synagogue mosaic at nearby Nirim (ancient Ma'on). The design and execution of the two mosaics are almost identical, except that the synagogue mosaic is decorated with Jewish symbols and includes a Hebrew inscription.

stairs we found at Capernaum.

Around the synagogue proper were auxiliary rooms, a covered entrance porch or vestibule and a rather large courtyard. In the center of the courtyard was a place for ritual washing before prayer.

Adjacent to the apse and to the left of it, are the remains of a stone structure which was built on top of the mosaic. This structure was the *bema* or dais from which the portion of the Law was read. Since it is on top of the mosaic, we may conclude that it was placed here after the mosaic was laid and was not a part of the original structure.

Beth-Alpha—A plan of the synagogue showing the location of the various parts of the elaborate mosaics.

Few ancient *bemot* have survived. Scholars speculate that this was because most of them were made of wood, rather than stone. The few stone *bemot*, or vestiges of *bemot*, that have been found suggest that the *bema* was probably adjacent to the Torah shrine rather than in the center of the prayer hall as is often the case in orthodox synagogues even today. The most complete antique *bema* ever found, carved from a single block of stone, comes from Aleppo in Syria. Unfortunately, the building had been converted into a mosque—a not uncommon conversion after the Moslem conquest—and the *bema* was not found *in situ*. The *bema* was approached by three steps, and the holes in the top of the *bema* indicate it was surrounded by a balustrade. Its Jewish character is attested by a Hebrew inscription carved into it.

The *bema* frequently bore inscriptions. At Sussiya, a large number of marble inscriptional fragments were found. The excavators tell us these fragments were once part of marble slabs that provided the facing of the *bema*. The slabs contained flowers, birds and tendrils carved in openwork technique. Around this was a plain band which contained inscriptions recording the names of donors. Above the plain band were freestanding floral decorations.

Returning to Beth Alpha, the entire synagogue compound was paved with mosaics. The synagogue was destroyed in an earthquake in the sixth century. First, a layer of plaster fell from the roof and walls onto the mosaic and formed a protective cover against the stonework which tumbled down when the building collapsed. Because of the protective covering of plaster, the mosaics are in an excellent state of preservation.

The most spectacular of the Beth Alpha mosaics is in the nave of the synagogue room. It consists of three horizontal panels within a border.

The upper panel, adjacent to the apse which housed the Torah ark, is a traditional and typical synagogue scene in synagogue art. In the center is the *aron ha-kodesh*, the Ark of the Law, with its panelled doors closed. Above the ark is a pointed gable and inside the gable is a decorative shell over which hangs the *ner tamid*, or eternal light. Lions guard either side of the ark and above them are two three-footed *menorot*. Filling up the space—in conformity with the Byzantine *horror vacui*—are the usual ritual objects: *shofar*, *lulav*, *etrog*, and incense shovel. Two large birds which look like ostriches stand on projections from the ark. On either end of the

opposite
Hammath-Tiberias—The three-panelled mosaic, now broken by a later wall. The upper panel contains a Torah ark flanked by *menorot* and the center panel contains a zodiac; Beth Alpha has similar features. The superb talent of the mosaicist at Hammath-Tiberias, however, stands in marked contrast to the folk artist at Beth Alpha. Hammath-Tiberias was obviously a center of culture. The bottom panel contains lions facing nine Greek inscriptions, which honor the founders of the synagogue.

panel—although it is fully seen only on the right side—is a curtain drawn back to expose the Ark of the Law. Note that the curtain does not simply cover the Ark of the Law as in modern and some ancient synagogues; it covers the entire apse area. Perhaps, by this time, the curtain replaced the apse screen as the device to separate the congregation from the sacred area of the Torah.

The lowest panel of the mosaic, which greets the visitor on entering the synagogue, portrays a scene from the Bible—the binding of Isaac. On the left, are Abraham's two servants and their saddled donkey with a bell tied around its neck. Next is the ram caught in the thicket which God provided to replace the child sacrifice of Isaac. Further to the right stands father

Abraham, his beard streaked with gray, his sacrifical knife drawn, holding[25] his son Isaac in his other hand, ready to place him on the altar whose flames leap up to complete the picture. Both Abraham and Isaac, are labelled in Hebrew letters. Above the ram is a Hebrew inscription, "And behold the ram." But the surprise is the hand of God himself which is portrayed in the mosaic as coming down from heaven, extending from a cloud which shields the sun and whose rays can be clearly seen. Beside the hand is a quotation in Hebrew from the Bible: "Lay not . . ." The complete biblical sentence is "Lay not thy hand on the lad."

It would be difficult to exaggerate the astonishment which greeted the discovery of a portrayal of the hand of God in a synagogue—and on the floor yet, for all to walk on when entering the prayer hall. It is an interesting sidelight that during the period when the Beth Alpha mosaic was laid, the church was far more restrictive than the synagogue in what was per-

Hammath-Tiberias—This graceful naked youth represents a sign of the zodiac. Were it not so common, we would be surprised to find it on the floor of a synagogue located at the center of Jewish culture.

Beth Shean—This mosaic contains two Torah arks, one within the other. The outer one is capped by a triangular pediment. From the topmost point of the pediment a lamp originally hung, but only a few tesserae of the lamp and the chain from which the lamp hung remains. The inner Torah ark is capped by a semi-circular pediment housing a shell. A *paroket* or curtain hangs in front of the ark, rather than the panelled doors which we usually see. On either side of the ark is a *menorah* and a realistically depicted *shofar* and incense shovel.

mitted to be portrayed. In 427 C.E. even the use of the cross was forbidden on pavements.[26]

The biggest surprise in the Beth Alpha mosaic is in the large central panel, for here we find a thoroughly pagan zodiac. Around the zodiac circle are the signs of each of the months, each sign with its label in Hebrew. In the four corners are pictures of the four seasons, portrayed as winged cherubs. In the center the Greek sun-god Helios rides a chariot drawn by four galloping horses. Here is excavator E. L. Sukenik's own dramatic description of Helios and his chariot:

The picture portrays the most important moment in the sun's circuit, as it rises out of the darkness of night. The dim skies are still sprinkled with stars, and among the stars which here and there appear in the heavens is seen the crescent moon. But the stars are gradually sinking, and already most of them are low on the horizon beneath the Chariot of the Sun. In the upper part of the circle, set on the long full neck, emerges the full, pink face of the Youthful Sun. Golden locks grace his head which is surrounded with an orb of light, branching out into seven rays.[27]

Thus we have come full circle, all the way from a geometric carpet at Aegina to a portrait of the sun god Helios. We shall reserve discussion of what it all means for later chapters.

One final point about the Beth Alpha mosaic. Shocking though its representations may be to some, none of its elements is unique. For example, at Hammath-Tiberias recent excavations have disclosed a beautifully preserved mosaic portraying not only an Ark of the Law flanked by *menorot* (incidentally, the curtain here covers only the Ark of the Law, not the whole apse), but also a zodiac with Helios in the center. Indeed, the zodiac is re-

129

peated in four or five ancient synagogues. And even the hand of God at Beth Alpha is not unique; it exists hundreds of miles away at Dura-Europos.

Beth Alpha cannot be explained as just an aberration. It is part of a tradition.

Hammath-Tiberias—The sun and its rays frame this sensitively executed Helios from the center of the zodiac. Dressed in Greek garb, he holds a shield and a whip in his left hand.

9 ✡ OUT IN THE FIELD

Excavating a synagogue in layers

The number of unexcavated archaeological sites in the Land of Israel runs into the many hundreds. The problem is not finding a site worth excavating, but finding the time and money. Often a site is chosen only because it is about to become unavailable to the scientific world unless promptly excavated—a building is about to be constructed on top of it; or some Bedouins found a tomb and the contents are being looted and sold on the black market. Then the archaeologists rush in to obtain from the site all that can be gleaned by a scientific archaeological expedition.

In a way, that is how the post-Roman town of Ein-Gedi happened to be excavated. In 1968 a rumor reached Jerusalem that the Ein-Gedi kibbutz was about to plant a grove of date palms on a site where, not long before, a nearby nature field school had discovered a tiny patch of ancient mosaic. If the site were plowed up and planted, that would mean the site would be unavailable to the archaeologists for decades at least. If they wanted to excavate, they would have to act now.

The rumor was false. It was floated by the field school which was fascinated by the patch of mosaic and wanted it excavated. (The kibbutz had attempted to sow the site, but found it unsuitable for planting because of the stones.)

All this was unknown to Professor Benjamin Mazar of The Hebrew University when the rumor of the "about-to-be-planted" palm grove reached him. The rumor was meant for his ears because he had excavated a Chalcolithic site on the heights above the Ein-Gedi kibbutz gardens, as well as a late Iron Age mound near the mosaic patch found by the field school. Ein-Gedi was, so to speak, archaeologically his; if more digging was to be done at Ein-Gedi, Mazar would make the decision.

In 1968, Mazar had already begun a major new excavation at the Temple Mount in Jerusalem. He had no time to return to Ein-Gedi. However, believing the rumor to be true, Mazar asked two young scholars to investigate the site, do some preliminary soundings, and if advisable, undertake a full-scale excavation. The two young men Mazar approached were Dan Barag of The Hebrew University and Yosef Porat of the Israel Department of Antiquities. These two men subsequently became director and deputy director of new Ein-Gedi excavations.

Ein-Gedi lies on the western shore of the Dead Sea amidst desolate surroundings of the Judean wilderness. Ein-Gedi itself is an oasis situated at the confluence of two *wadis* or dry river beds that wind through the mountains. In these two *wadis* are springs (they are referred to in the Bible) which flow toward the Dead Sea. Here David fled from King Saul's wrath; and visitors today can still see caves in the hills like the ones in which young David hid. The two *wadis* of Ein-Gedi come together in a fertile plain that at various times in antiquity flourished with date palms, balsam and other medicinal and aromatic plants. The site appears to have been abandoned for the most part from about the 7th century C.E. until modern times, when the present Ein-Gedi kibbutz was established after Israel became a state. Today it is one of the most beautiful and prosperous *kibbutzim* in all Israel, a green jewel in the midst of the desert.

When Dan Barag arrived at Ein-Gedi and dusted off that patch of mosaic, he suddenly remembered a conversation he had had with Professor Mazar several years before, while Mazar had been excavating at Ein-Gedi. The two men, professor and student, were discussing a literary reference to Ein-Gedi in the ecclesiastical history of one of the early Church

Ein-Gedi—A view of the synagogue with the kibbutz in the background and the Dead Sea in the upper right. On the other side of the Dead Sea are the mountains of Moab, now in Jordan. To the left of the man in the distance are the rectangular wall stubs of the Torah shrine.

Ein-Gedi—The peacock mosaic from the later synagogue. The center peacocks are enclosed in two rectangles, a diamond and a circle. Pairs of peacocks with a bunch of grapes are in each corner of the outer rectangle.

Fathers, Eusebius, who wrote in the 4th century C.E. According to Eusebius, there was a very large Jewish village at Ein-Gedi. "Surely a large Jewish village must have had a synagogue," Barag told his professor. "Where is it?" the student asked. Mazar jerked his head back and raised his eyebrows in a typical Israeli gesture that says both "I don't know" and "I wish I knew."

As Dan Barag looked at the patch of mosaic, he wondered if this was the synagogue floor. Since the village was probably not prosperous enough to have used mosaic floors in private houses the mosaic must have been in a public building, most likely a synagogue. The more difficult question was whether the mosaic was in a courtyard to the synagogue or in the main synagogue room. Proceeding on a hunch that they were in the main synagogue room, Barag and Porat sunk a trench in what they hoped would be the north wall of the synagogue, the one facing Jerusalem. They were right. In a few weeks, a beautiful Torah shrine appeared in the middle of the north wall of the room and the building's identification as a synagogue was confirmed.

In their first season at Ein-Gedi in 1968, the excavators uncovered most of the mosaic in the nave of the synagogue room, one of the most beautiful floors ever found in a synagogue. A geometrical design in the center of the floor consisting of two rectangles, a diamond and a circle, all within one another, encloses two pairs of birds. The corners of the outer rectangle are decorated with pairs of peacocks and bunches of grapes. In-

133

Ein-Gedi—The bronze *menorah* (after cleaning) found inside the synagogue, near the Torah shrine.

Ein-Gedi—Byzantine coins wrapped in linen help date the synagogue's destruction. The coins date from the mid-sixth century C.E.

right
Ein-Gedi—One of the largest synagogue inscriptions ever discovered (smaller, however, than the Rehov inscription—see pages 46-47), uncovered in the western aisle of the Ein-Gedi synagogue. The inscription includes quotations from the Bible, a literary zodiac and curses on those who would divide the community.

side the circle are four more birds. The spaces are filled with lovely and unusual designs. The archaeologists also uncovered on the mosaic floor of the western aisle of the synagogue room four Hebrew and Aramaic inscriptions (in the next season they found a fifth). These inscriptions included quotations from the Bible, commemorations of donors to the synagogue building, curses on those who would divide the community or pass on malicious tales to the gentiles, and a literary zodiac (that is, a description rather than a depiction). Near the Ark of the Law, they found a unique *menorah*, cast in bronze, which was no doubt used during the service. Another unique find near the Ark of the Law was a charred wooden disc, one of the roller ends for the Torah Scroll. This is the only such disc ever recovered from antiquity.

But the first season left many questions unanswered. What was the

opposite
Ein-Gedi—The bronze *menorah in situ.*

architectural history of the building? What were the stages of its use? When was it built? When was it destroyed? What kinds of buildings surrounded the synagogue? How did they relate to the synagogue? It was to these questions that the second and third seasons of excavation were devoted.

Fixing the date of the destruction of the latest synagogue at Ein-Gedi proved relatively easy. Beneath the debris and dirt which accumulated from sporadic medieval and Bedouin habitation of the site (which was first removed by the excavators) was a layer of ash which attested to a violent conflagration. The fire had apparently been fiercest in the area of the Ark of the Law, where much wood and parchment—from the Ark, the Torah Scrolls and a genizah behind the Ark—fed the fire. In one of the private houses near the synagogue, the excavators found in the same strata of ash a purse of coins tightly wrapped in a piece of linen. In the course of the violent fire, the owner of the coins could not get back to the house to collect them. These coins could be dated; and thus they provided the time-frame for the destruction of the Ein-Gedi synagogue—the mid-sixth century C.E. This date was confirmed by a hoard of coins found in the genizah of the synagogue, the latest of which dated to the same period. Had the fire been accidental, reasons Barag, the synagogue would have been re-built, not abandoned. Barag speculates that the town was set to fire in the mid-6th century as part of Justinian's persecution of the Jews.

When the synagogue was built proved to be a more difficult and still not completely solved problem. The question is complicated by the fact that the excavators soon discovered they were dealing not with a single synagogue, but with at least two synagogues, one on top of the other, a rather frequent occurrence in synagogue excavation. They would have to try to date the earlier synagogue or synagogues as well. Vivid evidence of an earlier synagogue was uncovered at the end of the second season when the peacock mosaic floor was lifted so that it could be taken to Jerusalem for repair and conservation. Underneath was another completely preserved mosaic floor!

Before the startled eyes of the assembled archaeologists a series of mosaic squares were found, the most prominent of which contained a large swastika. The swastika, like the six-pointed star, is a geometric design widely distributed in antiquity. It appears in Jewish art and occasionally in synagogues as well (as, for example, the swastikas with rounded arms in the synagogue on the Greek isle of Aegina[1]). But never before had the swastika been given such prominence as at Ein-Gedi. (Prior to the Nazi era, swastikas were not confined to *ancient* synagogues. After Hitler came to power congregants of the Emmanuel Synagogue of Hartford, Connecticut discovered to their horror that the synagogue vestibule had been paved with a mosaic containing several swastikas. The mosaic pavement was promptly ripped out.)

Beneath the later peacock mosaic floor, but on top of the swastika floor, the archaeologists found column bases. Column bases would not be expected on top of a mosaic floor if the columns had been put in at the same time as the mosaic floor. Rather we would expect the mosaic floor to be laid around the column bases. Because the column bases in this case were on top of the swastika mosaic floor, the archaeologists reasoned that the earlier synagogue must have had two phases: the first a columnless building; the second, using the same swastika floor, with columns erected on top. Then, some time afterward, the synagogue was rebuilt and the new peacock mosaic floor was laid over the old one.

With the help of the expedition's architect, Ehud Netzer, the archaeologists were able to correlate these changes in the floor with changes in the walls and especially in the north wall which contained the Torah shrine.

In the first phase of the earlier building the entrance to the synagogue was on the north wall. In this building, there was no permanent Torah shrine—just as in the early basilica-plan synagogues in the Galilee. The entrance facade on the north side faced Jerusalem. The Ark of the Law was brought in for the service in a portable chest, which the worshippers faced.

In the second phase of the earlier building, columns were placed on the swastika mosaic floor to support what was probably a new roof. The center entrance to the synagogue on the north wall was blocked up by a row of mudbrick narrower than the wall itself, thus forming a small, but permanent Torah niche. The building could then be entered through one or possibly two doors—on either side of the now-blocked center entrance. This, however, became a secondary entrance. The principal entrance was through a columned portico added on the western side of the building. Three new doors were cut into the synagogue's eastern wall.

Earlier Building—Phase I

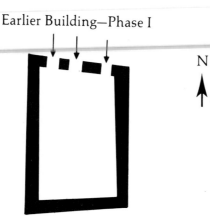

N

Earlier Building—Phase II

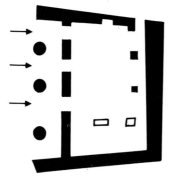

At a later date, a new synagogue was built on top of the old one and the new peacock mosaic floor was laid atop the old swastika floor. In addition, the portico was closed in and a narthex or entrance hall was added on the western side of the synagogue. The narthex was entered by a door at either end. But the most important change was in the Torah shrine. In this later building, a new Torah shrine was built out from, and in front of, the north wall. In the side of the Torah shrine facing the congregation was a niche for the Ark of the Law. Behind this was an area for storage—a genizah*—in the charred ruins of which were found the ashes of numerous Torah parchments and the disc which once formed part of the Torah roller. In front of the niche for the Torah ark was a *bema* containing its own mosaic floor.

Later Building

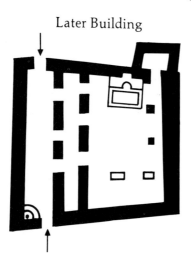

*Not to be confused with the additional room added on the back of the building.

Ein-Gedi—The Torah shrine with *bema*. Behind this installation (in the center of the picture) is a break in the wall which, during the first phase of the earlier synagogue, was an entrance to the synagogue. This entrance was partially filled in with mud brick during the earlier synagogue's second phase. That part of the wall which remained unfilled created a small niche, about half the width of the wall, for the Torah. When the later synagogue was built, the installation in front of the wall (to house the Torah ark) was added. Between the wall and the Torah ark is an empty space that probably served as a genizah where synagogue equipment and worn scrolls were kept. The stones just behind the rectangular stub of walls are shaped in the form of a semi-circle and formed the base of the Torah ark. In front of this is the *bema* which originally had a mosaic floor.

Just inside the south entrance to the narthex was discovered a beautifully preserved *kiyor* or basin for washing hands and feet before prayer, the first time one of these installations has been found in an excavation. The drain for carrying the dirty water away may still be seen. Nearby was found a lovely two handled jar from which the water was probably poured into the *kiyor*.

To determine when the synagogue with the swastika floor was built, Dr. Barag dug a section beneath the swastika floor. There he found another destruction layer. Prior to the Roman destruction of Jerusalem in 70 C.E., Ein-Gedi was under direct Roman administration—a kind of crown estate—because of its valuable balsam and other medicinal plants. It was attacked and plundered on Passover night in 68 C.E. by the Zealots of Masada, as recounted by the Jewish historian Josephus, in the Zealots' desperate effort to throw off the Roman yoke. Dr. Barag thinks the destruction level below the swastika mosaic floor is probably the destruction of Ein-Gedi by the Masada Zealots. So the Ein-Gedi synagogue as we know it so far was probably built sometime after the Roman destruction of Jerusalem. How long after is difficult to tell. Dr. Barag suggests sometime in the early third century. The synagogue was destroyed, as we saw, sometime in the mid-sixth century. During this period the building went through three stages, the earlier building with the swastika floor consisting of two phases and the later building with its peacock mosaic floor and elaborate Torah shrine.

But that is not the end of the story of the Ein-Gedi synagogue. The end of the story cannot yet be written. Dan Barag and his team of archaeolo-

gists would like to return to Ein-Gedi for at least one, and perhaps several, more seasons of digging. Many intriguing questions remain to be answered.

What were the Jews of Ein-Gedi like? Their houses are all around the synagogue, yet not a single complete house has been excavated. Why were their beautiful mosaics—situated far from the centers of Hellenistic culture in the Galilee—devoid of human forms? Is there information still buried that will help to date the three phases of the Ein-Gedi synagogue more accurately? Is there other evidence of Jewish observance to be found?

But the big question is, what lies beneath the Ein-Gedi synagogue? Does another synagogue lie below the swastika mosaic floor? If so, it is likely to be a synagogue that preceded the destruction of the Second Temple in 70 C.E. There are tantalizing reasons for believing that such a synagogue is there. We know from archaeological as well as literary evidence that synagogues were in existence before the destruction of the Second Temple; indeed, two such buildings—at Masada and Herodium—have been found. We also know that synagogues seldom move around within a town. Synagogue land was owned by the community, so it was rarely transferred. Thus, if there was a Jewish community living in this part of Ein-Gedi in the days before the destruction of the Second Temple, it is likely that their synagogue is lying undiscovered beneath the swastika mosaic floor.

One final comment must be made about the Ein-Gedi synagogue. As the reader may have noticed, we have made no effort to categorize the Ein-Gedi synagogue as a basilica-plan, a broadhouse-plan or an apse-plan synagogue. That is because it does not fit any of these neat categories which

Ein-Gedi—An overview of the excavation. The synagogue is the large room at center left. The peacock mosaic is in the center of the synagogue. The upper left-hand part of the synagogue has been destroyed. In the upper right-hand corner of the room benches are preserved. Similar benches probably once lined all the walls of this room. At the bottom of the synagogue is the outline of the Torah shrine and *bema*. On the right side of the synagogue (below the benches) are three entrances which were created in the second phase of the earlier synagogue. These three entrances lead, on the right, to the western aisle where the long inscription was found. Further to the right is a narthex or entrance hall added when the later synagogue was built. Then the synagogue was entered from either end of this long hall. In the upper right corner of this hall can be seen the *kiyor* or washing basin. Around the synagogue are private houses.

scholars have created. It is neither a basilica-plan, nor a broadhouse-plan nor an apse-plan synagogue.[2] The lesson to be learned from this is that just as the end of the story of the Ein-Gedi synagogue cannot be written, neither can the definitive story of ancient synagogues be written. The three types of synagogues that we have been discussing in this book are only ways of organizing what we know about ancient synagogues. The plan of the Ein-Gedi synagogue, which does not fit into any of these categories, only emphasizes how much we don't know, how much we have yet to learn. Perhaps someday we will have to abandon these categories as no longer useful. Perhaps new categories will be devised that more meaningfully organize our knowledge about ancient synagogues. In any event, the Ein-Gedi synagogue reminds us how tentative our knowledge is.

We have concentrated on the Ein-Gedi synagogue in this chapter in order to give some idea of the thrill and excitement involved in excavating an ancient synagogue, and to emphasize that new knowledge is being uncovered all the time. However, Ein-Gedi is not the only synagogue excavation that is still in progress. There are a number of other excavations that might as easily have been chosen as the subject for this chapter. For example, Dan Bahat of the Israel Department of Antiquities is, as I write, excavating a synagogue at Beth Shean in the Jezreel Valley. Three young American scholars—Eric Meyers from Duke University, Thomas Kraabel from Wisconsin, and James Strange from Florida, are excavating two syna-

Ein-Gedi—In the upper left is one of the two entrances to the synagogue's narthex or entrance hall, a hall added when the later synagogue (with the peacock mosaic) was built. The floor of the entrance is a plain mosaic without design of any kind. In the corner, just inside the entrance is a *kiyor* or water basin in which hands and feet were washed before prayer. The bowl and jug have been placed where they were found. They were probably used in connection with the *kiyor*. Notice the slant in the height of the *kiyor* so that the water would drain out in the right direction. At the base of the *kiyor* on the left is a water drainage hole in the wall, leading outside the synagogue.

gogues in northern Galilee, one at Shema and the other at Meiron. Later we shall look in some detail at the giant new synagogue recently uncovered at Sardis in Turkey, and another at Ostia near Rome. What all this archaeological activity will ultimately disclose, no one can tell. All we can be sure of is that the closer we think we are to the last word, the more likely we are to be surprised by what the archaeologists unearth.

10 ✡ THE IMAGE
IN THE SYNAGOGUE

Or what ever happened to the
Second Commandment?

At the turn of the century, a Jewish scholar was asked to prepare an article on Jewish art. His reply was that he "could more easily write an apology for its non-existence."[1] The question he sought to answer was not whether there was a Jewish art, but, rather "why Israel has no art."[2] Until recently, it was supposed that there was no such thing as Jewish art, at least in antiquity.

In a famous and frequently-quoted passage, the distinguished art critic Bernard Berenson wrote, "The Jews . . . have displayed little talent for the visual, and almost none for the figure arts . . . To the Jews belonged the splendours and raptures of the word."[3]

The source of this artistic void was generally considered to be the Second Commandment[4] and other biblical passages forbidding the making of images and idols.[5] As Sigmund Freud said, "The prohibition against making an image of God . . . signified subordinating sense perception to an abstract idea."[6] In the exercise of building a fence around the Torah, the Jewish people sought to eliminate any temptation to transgress the commandment against idolatry by prohibiting the depiction of all human and animal forms; and thus the Jews became a people without visual arts.

For some critics, this biblical proscription against image-making was not adequate to account for the Jewish people's lack of artistic talent. They reasoned that even before the adoption of the prohibition, there must have been some innate artistic deficiency in a people which could accept so rigorous a hostility toward the reproduction of human and animal life in any guise whatever. In other words, it was not the biblical prohibition that caused the absence of art, but, rather, the absence of art that permitted the adoption of the biblical prohibition. Some scholars went even further and found that the Jew also had a defective sense of color: "Such a command as that of the Decalogue's [prohibition of images] would have been impossible to a nation possessed of such artistic gifts as the Greeks, and was carried to its ultimate consequences ... only because the [Jewish] people lacked artistic inclination, with its creative power and formative imagination .... The same reasons, to which is to be added a defective sense of color, prevented any development of painting." This is not a quotation from some nineteenth century anti-semite, but from the *Jewish Encyclopedia*, presenting a scholarly consensus.[7]

This attitude, or subtle atavistic variations of it, persisted into the twentieth century. For example, a Jewish scholar writing in 1946 tells us that the Jew "does not see as clearly as he hears."[8]

In 1950 an Oxford scholar wrote in *Commentary* magazine, a publication of the American Jewish Committee, that the Second Commandment "has been understood by the Jewish people themselves as a prohibition against representation irrespective of its purpose—a kind of general exclusion of delight in art. As a result, in the field of the visual arts, Jewish genius suffered a thwarting that was self-imposed, and hence all the more damaging."[9]

Underlying this quotation, as well as the entire body of literature which attempts to explain the lack of Jewish art, is the belief that the Second Commandment effectively prevented any significant Jewish artistic endeavor. As one writer stated, "The essence of the prohibition was observed in most Jewish communities at most times; and where and when individuals freed themselves of it, they lost touch with their people."[10] Surveys of the sources concluded that "representations of the human countenance were strictly prohibited and rigorously excluded everywhere."[11] "The great leaders of the Jewish race have ever been opposed to the artistic representation of natural forms."[12] Citations to the first century Jewish historian Josephus, the contemporaneous Jewish philosopher Philo, and the Talmud were used to support the supposition that observant Jews did not tolerate the depiction of human and animal forms. A favorite talmudic reference

Three-dimensional cherubim with outspread wings above the ark of the law are described in the Bible and are depicted here in an engraving from an early 18th century Dutch Bible.

This imaginary representation of the great bronze basin in Solomon's temple comes from an early 18th century Dutch Bible. The biblical text does not condemn, as a violation of the Second Commandment, the representation of the twelve oxen on which the basin is mounted.

was the passage which recounted how a pious Jew even avoided gazing at the pictures engraved on Roman coins.[13]

However, in the past 50 years or so, archaeological excavations have uncovered a wealth of Jewish art, heretofore unknown to scholars. As a result, any argument about the lack of Jewish art has been demolished. Now unearthed for all to view, the facts have once again confounded the scholars and it is no longer possible to base an argument on the absence of human and animal forms in Jewish art. Much of this evidence comes from the synagogues we have looked at. Additional evidence comes from funerary remains—tombs, catacombs, ossuaries, and sarcophagi. All of this attests to a rich and varied Jewish art during the early centuries of the Common Era.

In the light of this plethora of evidence, scholars have had to rework their histories and theories. And in these modern scholarly writings, they call our attention to a number of biblical instances in which images were permitted and obviously approved by the biblical writer. Thus, the restriction on images, we are now told, was not as uniform as was once supposed. For example, the biblical craftsman, Bezalel, under the direction of no less a figure than Moses, placed two three-dimensional cherubim with wings outspread above the Ark of the Law itself.[14] The great bronze basin in Solomon's Temple was mounted on twelve bronze oxen; and the Temple itself was decorated with lions and carved cherubim.[15] The restored Temple of Ezekiel's vision was decorated not only with the faces of lions but also those of men.[16] Surely those leaders who canonized these passages of the Bible in the Second Temple period found them to be unobjectionable, despite the use of the images they describe.

In a brilliant study, Rabbi Joseph Gutmann has analyzed the context in which both Josephus and Philo wrote in order to explain why both of them attribute to the Jews of the late Second Temple period a far more intense antipathy toward representational art than was probably in fact the case.[17] Josephus, the commander of the Jewish forces in the Galilee during the first Jewish revolt against Rome which began in 66 C.E., deserted to the Romans when he thought the Jewish cause seemed hopeless. Writing his Jewish history from Rome, he sought to explain the Jewish hatred of Rome on a religious basis, rather than on a political one. Thus, according to Josephus, an insurrection that nearly broke out when Herod installed a Roman eagle above the great gate of the Temple Compound was not because of political hatred for Rome, but because the eagle offended Jewish religious sensibilities tutored on the Second Commandment.[18] The truth is, says Rabbi Gutmann, that Herod doubtless had the advance approval of the religious authorities for the erection of the eagle which Herod dedicated to the Temple. But Josephus felt safer in attributing the Jewish outrage to exaggerated religious scruples than to the real cause—hatred of Rome. Josephus offers a similar, and just as inaccurate, basis for Jewish reaction to Roman soldiers marching through the streets with the Roman standard containing an image of the emperor. According to Josephus, writing under the watchful eye of his Roman sponsors, the image, not the hated soldiers, was offensive to the Jews. Rabbi Gutmann also shows that Philo's philosophical condemnation of images is based more on his devotion to the Greek philosopher Plato, for whom the arts stood low, than on the Bible. For Philo, as for Plato, the image was an obstacle to philosophic truth which served to condemn images far more importantly than the fact that they might have constituted a violation of biblical law. As to the actual practice of the time, the Second Temple *menorah*, depicted on the Arch of Titus in Rome erected to commemorate the fall of Jerusalem, indicates the Temple *menorah* itself might have been decorated with sea horses in relief.[19]

In light of the new archaeological evidence for the use of images in synagogues, as well as other Jewish art in the post-Second Temple period, scholars looked anew not only at the Bible, but also at that great repository of what was thought to be rabbinic conservatism, the Talmud. In the Talmud, scholars have found that in addition to the fact that certain pious Jews avoided even looking at the images on Roman coins, there were other Jews (including the pious leaders of the academy of Nehardea in Babylonia, such as Rab and Samuel) who saw no objection to praying in a synagogue that contained a royal statue.[20]

Modern scholarship recovered a long lost passage of the Talmud which indicated that as early as the fourth century rabbis permitted mosaics to be used on synagogue floors. The passage was lost centuries ago as a result of what scholars call homoeoteleuton, a word that is almost as difficult to define abstractly as it is to pronounce. However, the process may be described quite simply. It has surely occurred to everyone who has typed a lengthy manuscript. You look up for a moment, having just typed, let us say, the word "prohibition." You look down again for the word "prohibition" and your eye alights on the word, not where you left off typing but at another occurence of the word four lines later. Without realizing it, you begin typing at the second occurrence of the word. As a result, you have omitted everything between the first and second occurrence of the word. It occurs not infrequently in the transmission of ancient manuscripts, as well as in the typing of modern ones. Professor J.N. Epstein, while examining an ancient copy of the Palestinian Talmud in the State Library of Leningrad, discovered a passage which had been omitted from the standard text

Triumphant Romans marching with the Temple *menorah* and other Temple spoils after the fall of Jerusalem in 70 C.E., as depicted on the Arch of Titus in Rome. Six horses appear in relief on the *menorah's* unusual octagonal base rather than the customary plain three-footed stand; scholars disagree as to whether the base is authentic.

of the Talmud as a result of an ancient scribal homoeoteleuton. The omitted passage read as follows: "In the days of Rabbi Abun they began to depict designs on mosaics, and he did not hinder them"[21] Rabbi Abun is known to have lived in the first half of the fourth century.[22] According to Professor E.L. Sukenik, "to depict designs," as used in the omitted passage, means "to make representations of living creatures." Here is talmudic toleration, if not permission, albeit long unknown, for the use of living creatures in synagogue mosaic floors. An almost identical passage also allows paintings in synagogues.[23]

In a series of articles, a leading Israeli talmudist, Professor E.E. Urbach, found a number of largely ignored passages in which the Talmud text reflected a far more tolerant attitude toward the use of images than was hitherto supposed.[24] For example, the Talmud interprets the passage in *Deuteronomy 7* which requires the burning of graven images as meaning: "That which is *treated* as a god is forbidden, but that which is not *treated* as a god is permitted." Professor Urbach excoriated those scholars, "who are accustomed to a one-sided view of the history of *Halachah*, seeing in it only an accumulation of increasingly severe and increasingly numerous legal safeguards."[25]

The rabbinical literature reflects a wide variety of opinions regarding the proscription against images, according to Professor Urbach; in most cases,

147

the Talmud reflects a realistic approach to actual problems. Indeed, as Urbach points out, some rabbis even permitted Jews to make and market idols to the heathen, provided the Jews themselves did not worship them. In light of this ruling, it is hardly surprising to find liberal talmudic interpretations of these same biblical provisions as applied to synagogue art.

A similar situation is found in other rabbinic literature. In *Targum Jonathan*, an Aramaic paraphrase of the Bible, we read that *Leviticus* 26:1 tells us that we may not set up a figured stone, to bow down to it, "but a mosaic pavement of designs and forms," says the *Targum*, "you may set in the floor of your places of worship, so long as you do not do obeisance to it."

Thus it now appears that the attitude toward representational art varied from time to time, from place to place and even from rabbi to rabbi; and all purported to follow the biblical text.

It is not difficult to give the biblical text more than one interpretation. The principal ambiguity lies in the fact that every biblical prohibition of images also relates to the prohibition of idolatry. The Second Commandment may serve as an example:

You shall not make for yourself a graven image, or any likeness of anything that is in the heaven above, or that is on the earth beneath, or that is in the water under the earth; you shall not bow down to them or serve them. (Exodus 20:4-5; Deuteronomy 5:4-5)

The part of the quotation *before* the semi-colon can be interpreted as an absolute prohibition against human and animal figures.* The part of the quotation *after* the semi-colon emphasizes that the prohibited images and likenesses must not be served or bowed down to. That is, they must not be treated as idols. A liberal interpretation is that the prohibition of the commandment is aimed at images and likeness used as idols, not at images and likenesses which are not so used. Thus if the image is not worshipped, it does not come within the proscription of the comandment.

In late Roman times and during the Byzantine period, idolatry was no longer the problem it was in the days of King Ahab or even during the 7th century B.C.E. reforms of King Josiah. As Saul Lieberman has pointed out, "In the first centuries C.E. the Jews were so far removed from clear-cut idolatry that there was not the slightest need to argue and to preach against it."[27] Once the threat of idolatry abated, the prohibition of images could be relaxed. An interpretation of the Second Commandment which emphasized its relation to idolatry easily formed the basis for relaxing it.

This is not to say that all rabbinical authorities took this liberal view. But a careful reading of the rabbinical literature reflects a wide divergence of opinion as to the nature of permitted representation—from the severely restricted to the permissive—and all within the traditional bounds of normative Judaism.

---

*However even here there are some ambiguities. For example, the Hebrew text of the Second Commandment is not precisely the same in *Exodus* and *Deuteronomy*. One text can be read as prohibiting "a graven image *or* any likeness," and the other "a graven image *of* any likeness;" the latter prohibition, it can be argued, is confined to three-dimensional representations.[26] While there is abundant archaeological evidence for relief carvings, there appears to have been little Jewish sculpture in the round. But there is some. For example, the head of a lion was found at Chorazim and at Bar-Am; and, as we shall see, three-dimensional lions were also used at Sardis.

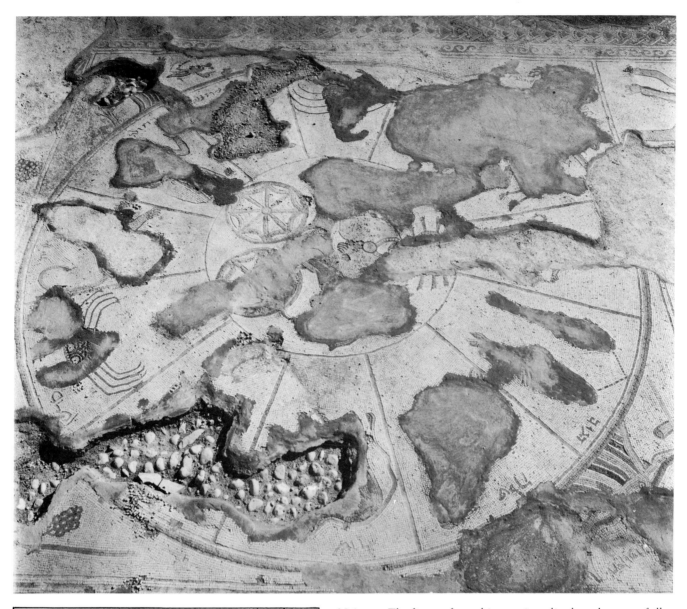

Na'aran—The figures from this mosaic zodiac have been carefully gouged out by an iconoclast who was offended by the "images". Many of the Hebrew names of the zodiac signs can still be seen. In the center of the zodiac was the Greek god Helios in his chariot. As the picture was taken from the side, the two chariot wheels are seen one above the other on the left side of the center circle. Helios' face has been destroyed, but some of the rays from his head are visible on the right side of the center circle.

Na'aran—A line drawing of the zodiac's remains helps to identify the elements in the photograph.

Na´aran—In addition to the zodiac and Helios depicted in his chariot, this synagogue mosaic included two *menorot* and a Torah ark.

Indeed, there were probably differences in attitude even within the same synagogue—we have evidence that such a difference may well have existed at Dura-Europos. This may be the explanation for the curious fact that the eyes have been carefully gouged out on figure after figure on the lowest register of paintings. An incident is recorded in the Talmud in which a rabbi demanded that the image on a seal be annulled by putting out its eyes. This may well reflect a common way of voiding the offending effect of prohibited images. The eyeless biblical paintings in the Dura-Europos synagogue may attest the work of those members of the congregation who objected to the images and who secretly annulled by disfigurement those figures on the lowest register which they could reach.

The Hasmonean legacy led to a strict attitude among the Jews prior to the destruction of the Second Temple in 70 C.E., as reflected in an almost complete lack of images in the archaeological materials of that period.[28] Thereafter, until about the end of the sixth century, there is no discernible pattern in the archaeological evidence as to the ways in which the prohibition against images was actually observed. Perhaps the lavish biblical scenes from Dura-Europos suggest a more liberal attitude in the diaspora than prevailed in Palestine. Perhaps the simple geometric design of the earlier Ein-Gedi synagogue suggests that areas less affected by Hellenistic culture were more conservative in this regard. But on the available evidence, it is difficult to know with certainty.

At the end of the sixth century, the archaeological evidence suggests that a conservative reaction began to set in. At the synagogue at Hamath-Gader we see lions, but no men in the mosaic floor. At Jericho, even the animals have disappeared and the representations are confined to ritual objects in a mosaic floor that complies with the strictest interpretation of the Second Commandment. Additional evidence for this conservative reaction may be seen in the iconoclasm we find in Palestinian synagogues. It was then, scholars believe, that the images were chiselled out in the Galilean synagogues and the animals were gouged out of the zodiac in the mosaic floor at the synagogue at Na´aran. At the same time, other figured mosaics were destroyed from east of the Jordan to Asia Minor.[29]

Curiously enough, in the opinion of the majority of scholars, this aniconic, or anti-image, reaction is attributable not to a stricter interpretation of the Second Commandment, but to two religious movements outside Judaism: the iconoclastic movement in Christianity and the rise of Islam with its strict prohibition of anything but geometric designs.[30] These widespread anti-image sentiments could not fail to affect the Jews. An anti-image attitude on the part of the Jews lasted far longer in Moslem countries than in Christian countries, which soon recovered from the excesses of the iconoclastic movement.

150

11 ✡ PAGAN SYMBOLS IN SYNAGOGUE ART

What's a Greek god doing in a synagogue?

In the last chapter, we tried to understand how varying interpretations of the biblical proscription against images permitted—and sometimes restricted—the use of human and animal representations in synagogue art. This explained from the point of view of religious law, the appearance, for example, of birds on the Ein-Gedi synagogue floor and, even more important, the various biblical scenes—Noah's ark at Jerash, the binding of Isaac at Beth Alpha, Daniel in the lions den at Sussiya, and the whole series of biblical paintings at Dura-Europos.

But there is a significant category of synagogue art outside the scope of the preceding explanation—such as the cupids and Roman eagles at Capernaum, the head of Medusa at Chorazim, and Helios in his chariot at Beth Alpha and elsewhere. These are more than just pictures or images. That the Second Commandment permits the depiction of an animal or human form so long as it is not worshipped does not explain the use of pagan symbols and even pagan gods in synagogue art. Indeed, the use of these symbols trenches on the explicit prohibition of the biblical commandment, on what may be described as its central thrust and core concern—namely idolatry. No matter how liberally the Second Commandment is interpreted, we must still recognize that these representations drawn from Greek and Roman mythology are not explained by this interpretation. In short, what are these pagan symbols and pagan gods doing in a synagogue?

Between 1905 and 1907, a team of German archaeologists financed by a Jewish millionaire from Berlin, made a survey and conducted some excavations of ancient synagogues in the Galilee. Their extensive report published in 1916 is still a classic in the field.[1] They were the first among many scholars to stumble in trying to explain the use of blatant pagan symbols in synagogue art. Since the Galilean synagogues to which their study was devoted could all be assigned to the late second and third century C.E., they explained the pagan art in these synagogues in terms of that particular time frame. Their preferred explanation was this: The Antonine and Severan Caesars who ruled in Rome during the late second and third centuries were so favorably inclined toward the Jews that they gave these synagogues as imperial gifts to the various Jewish communities in Galilee; naturally the buildings were heavily decorated in rich Graeco-Roman style; and the Jews, not wishing to appear ungrateful or guilty of contumely, accepted them graciously though some of the features offended their religious sensibilities; as soon as they were free to do so, the Jews destroyed the offending images.[2] It was an ingenious explanation, but unfortunately far-fetched. Aside from the inherent improbability that the memory of such munificent endowments on so large a scale would have left no trace in the extensive rabbinical literature of the period,[3] it was hardly adequate to explain the later pagan symbols which subsequent archaeologists found in synagogue floors laid long after Christianity became the official religion of the empire and Byzantium was openly hostile to Judaism.

This early explanation of pagan symbols in synagogue art was only one of several which subsequent discoveries thoroughly undermined. As Professor Urbach has said, "The archaeologists, who were at first astounded by their own discoveries, have continually had to revise their theories, since, as a rule, every fresh excavation disproved the previous conjectures."[4]

The most prominent of these attempts to account for the Graeco-Roman symbols in antique synagogues cannot be dismissed so easily. It holds no more promise of being correct, but, it is such a monumental effort and so overflowing with valid scholarship and insight, that even if we must reject its central thesis, we must nevertheless do so in awe and admiration and with gratitude for what it teaches us. I refer to Erwin R. Goodenough's *Jewish Symbols in the Greco-Roman Period*,[5] a thirteen-volume monument to a life of scholarship which must be the starting point for any effort to understand the meaning of these pagan symbols in Jewish art.

Professor Goodenough's central thesis is that side by side with rabbinic Judaism, as reflected primarily in talmudic literature, there existed another Judaism which was antagonistic to what eventually emerged as normative orthodox Judaism. For this reason, the rabbinical literature gives no hint of the existence of this "other" Judaism. This "other" Judaism Professor Goodenough inferred from the nature of the archaeological remains.

What was the nature of this "other" Judaism, which left the stage of history without a trace in rabbinical literature? According to Goodenough, it was a complex, mystical, salvational religion. It emphasized a mystical union with God during life on earth through which alone salvation was possible. (Professor Goodenough believed that only by taking over this "other" form of Judaism was Christianity able to become so rapidly hellenized despite its purely Jewish origin).

These "other" Jews were neither idolators nor disloyal to Judaism. To the contrary, they considered themselves loyal both to the Law and the observances of Judaism. Instead, they added something: "A mysticism that they superimposed upon their Jewish observances, and adopted as an integral part of their religion."[6]

While Goodenough finds literary evidence for this "other" Judaism in the Jewish philosopher Philo, he pays primary attention to the archaeological evidence unearthed in recent years. Goodenough collects and describes this archaeological evidence in minute detail—from synagogues, tombs and other burials, and from lamps, charms, coins, amulets and other artifacts. Nothing is too small or too obscure to escape his notice. And while synagogues are only a part of his concern, his catalogue of synagogues is still the best description compiled at the time he wrote.[7]

Goodenough interprets almost every element of decoration as a symbol in support of his central thesis: The vine, the lion, the eagle, the fish, rosettes, designs, scenes, arrangements, architecture, strictly Jewish symbols, such as the *menorah* and Torah ark, as well as pagan gods and mythological figures—all have symbolic significance for his mystical, salvational, "other" Judaism. The core of this symbolic language, according to Goodenough, was drawn from the cult of Dionysus and was widely understood in the Graeco-Roman world. This symbolic language current in the Graeco-Roman world was used both to express and to gratify the worshippers' hope for salvation by participation in the life of a deity which gave itself to sacrificial death. These "other" Jews took over some of these symbols, and engrafted them onto Judaism. They added to this symbolic language Jewish symbols of their own. On the other hand, the rabbis who spawned the talmudic literature were, in Goodenough's view, both anti-image and opposed to mysticism; with their God no union was possible and his Law forbade making images. Accordingly, the widespread use of these mystical symbols attests to a widespread mystical Judaism which was poles apart from what ultimately became normative Judaism. This "other" Judaism was "oriented in mysticism and the hope of life after death in a sense far beyond anything that appears in synagogue worship under rabbinic guidance."[8]

As one commentator has wrily remarked, "To judge from the archaeological evidence, rabbinic Judaism must have been, by comparison with the mystical type, a minor sect."[9]

There are many reasons to reject Goodenough's central thesis. One may note the curious fact that his "other" Judaism apparently left no imprint on Jewish ritual[10] and is not referred to in the extensive polemical litera-

Beth Shearim—Carved in the wall of this catacomb is a large *menorah* in relief.

153

ture of Judaism, nor, for that matter, in Christian polemics.[11] The particular difficulty with Goodenough's theory that is of special interest here involves archaeological evidence found at Beth Shearim on the southern slopes of lower Galilee. Some of this archaeological evidence had been unearthed before Goodenough wrote, but some of it was found only after he had formulated his thesis in the early volumes of his work. At Beth Shearim archaeologists uncovered, in addition to a synagogue, a massive Jewish necropolis carved underneath a hill. From the over 100 sarcophagi, wall carvings and inscriptions found here, we get a picture of Jewish life not unlike what we have seen in the synagogues already discussed. *Menorot*, *lulavs* and *etrogs*, and Torah arks abound. In addition, we find sarcophagi heavily adorned with rich ornamentation borrowed from the Graeco-Roman world—garlands, carved lions, shells, and human figures. On the end of

Beth Shearim—A lavish triple-arched entrance to one of the Jewish catacombs, which were dug beneath a hill between the 2nd and 4th centuries C.E.

Beth Shearim—A sarcophagus decorated with an eagle and a wreath. The lid appears to depict a cow.

one sarcophagus is a bearded face in relief which resembles the customary representation of a pagan deity much like the one found in the synagogue of Chorazim. The excavator of the sarcophagus, Professor Nachman Avigad of The Hebrew University could barely contain himself: "It is startling to find such a carving on a Jewish coffin."[12] Marble fragments were found which revealed Greek mythological scenes, one of which was identified as Amazons in combat with Greeks. Another sarcophagus contains a damaged though easily-recognizable portrayal of Leda and the swan. The swan is, of course, Zeus in disguise, who impregnated the mortal Leda to give birth to the twins Castor and Pollux. When this sarcophagus was first discovered in a Jewish cemetery, scholars were so shocked that they were inclined to regard it as an accidental intrusion.[13] However, by the end of the excavation, Professor Avigad drily remarked, "It was not exceptional . . . Beth Shearim was apparently a good customer for this kind of pagan sarcophagi."[14]

Most startling about these finds is that they were uncovered not in some

Greek city of the diaspora overrun with Hellenistic influence and controlled by this "other" Judaism, but rather in Palestine *in the very center of traditional Judaism*! When, after the failure of the second Jewish revolt under Bar Kochba, the focus of Jewish life shifted from Judea to the Galilee, Beth Shearim became an important center of orthodox Jewish learning. The great Patriarch Judah ha-Nasi, known in Jewish history simply as "Rabbi", made his residence at Beth Shearim toward the end of the second century. Here he compiled much of the *Mishnah*, the first great code of Judaism's oral law which even today forms the core of the Talmud. Here he was buried. Here too was the seat of the Patriarchate and the home of the Sanhedrin, the supreme Jewish council. No city of the time was more imbued with traditional orthodox Judaism than Beth Shearim. Moreover, the Beth Shearim necropolis was famous throughout Jewry. Since Jews were forbidden from entering Jerusalem (renamed Aelia Capitolina by Emperor Hadrian), Jews from all over the world wanted to be buried in the necropolis of Beth Shearim which was sanctified by the last remains of Rabbi himself. (There is a very good possibility that the archaeologists have found the catacomb in which this holy man and his sons were buried.)

Yet in the very center of traditional Judaism, in this necropolis where the most distinguished rabbinical families of the time were buried, we find the same pagan motifs out of which Goodenough formulated his "other" Judaism.

Professor Avigad has observed that burial at Beth Shearim was no doubt controlled by some kind of burial society which would certainly have rejected the many sarcophagi with pagan symbols had the symbols offended a substantial Jewish public.[15] But whatever the formalities, surely we would not expect to find these pagan symbols so prominently represented in traditional Judaism's holiest burial ground available if there were two distinct antithetic and antagonistic Jewish movements.

Even more recent excavations at Hamath-Tiberias makes the same point as the Beth Shearim necropolis. For Tiberias, like Beth Shearim, was a thoroughly Jewish city dominated by normative Judaism. About the mid-third century, the seat of the Patriarchate was moved to Tiberias and with it the Sanhedrin. A famous academy flourished here, and indeed, most of the Palestinian Talmud was written in Tiberias. Yet in the synagogue of Hamath-Tiberias, we find the same zodiac mosaic, with Helios at its center, which was earlier found at Beth Alpha and Na'aran. Even more damaging to Goodenough's thesis, however, is an inscription by one of the donors to the Hamath-Tiberias synagogue who identifies himself as the *triphos* of the most illustrious patriarchs who were residing hardly a mile away. Thus it appears that even members of the patriarchal family itself worshipped here. If this synagogue were indeed a representative of an "other", "mystical" Judaism opposed to orthodox Judaism, this synagogue would be like finding a Protestant church within the confines of Vatican City, as Professor Michael Avi-Yonah of The Hebrew University recently remarked.[16] "We can only conclude," says Professor Avi-Yonah, "that the alleged antagonism between 'mystic' and 'normative' Judaism is a later purely theoretical construct."[17]

The truth of the matter is that the schizophrenic split from which Judaism suffered, according to Goodenough, is of his own creation. The dichotomy between traditional rabbinic Judaism and hellenized or paganized Judaism is itself a myth.

Another distinguished commentator has concluded, "[Goodenough's] pandemic sacramental paganism was a fantasy; so was the interpretation of

Beth Shearim—Inside the catacombs, sarcophagi are strewn about.

pagan symbols based on it, and so was the empire-wide, antirabbinic, mystical Judaism, based on an interpretation of these symbols. All three are enormous exaggerations of elements which existed, but were rare, in early imperial times."[18]

Some other explanation must be found for the appearance of pagan symbols in synagogues. That explanation must accept the fact that these pagan symbols were found in synagogues which were in the mainstream of the Judaism of their day.

Some scholars, perhaps in overreaction to Goodenough's extreme position, have suggested that these pagan elements were "mere ornaments" or "meaningless decoration,"[19] that they were the exact opposite of symbols, without meaning, mere examples of decorative repertoire of the day. Goodenough scoffed at this position. Why, for example, do we find Helios and his chariot in four or five synagogues, and other mythological figures not at all? To say this is mere decoration is to throw up one's hands, to give no explanation.

The scholarly world as a whole has had an uncomfortable feeling about the "mere decoration" explanation. But thus far no single satisfactory answer to the problem has been found. What has emerged, strangely enough, finds much of its inspiration in Goodenough. For if Goodenough did not find the right answers, he assuredly asked the right questions. It was he who more than anyone else collected and analyzed the materials and provided the insights from which a less extreme, more eclectic explanation can be constructed. While almost unanimously rejecting Goodenough's central thesis regarding the existence of an "other" Judaism, the scholarly world has also nearly unanimously acknowledged its debt to this great scholar. Professor Morton Smith of Columbia University, who, as earlier quoted, condemned Goodenough's major contentions as "fantasies" and "enormous exaggerations" immediately followed this condemnation with these words of praise:

Soit. Columbus failed, too. But his failure revealed a new world, and so did Goodenough's . . . The extent and importance of the Jewish iconic material was practically unrealized before Goodenough's collection of it. Informed opinions of ancient Judaism can never, henceforth, be the same as they were before he published. So long as the subject is studied and the history of the study is preserved, his work will mark an epoch.[20]

Yet this statement is vague too.[21] Perhaps as specific as we can get is to say that Goodenough has forced us to open our eyes to the fact that the Judaism of the early centuries of the Common Era was a far more complex, varied—and, may one say, far richer?—institution than we had known.

As we have seen, even the traditional rabbinical literature reveals a more varied attitude toward images than was once supposed. We recognize that the Talmud is not simply a *code* of laws; it preserves the arguments, the conflicting rulings and the dissents. Rabbinic Judaism was no monolith. There were those pious souls who refused to look at the image on a Roman coin while there were rabbis who approved the Jewish manufacture of idols for the pagans, so long as the idols were not worshipped by Jews. There were doubtless rabbis who insisted on limiting the decoration in their synagogues to geometric designs as at Ein-Gedi and Aegina in accordance with a strict interpretation of the Second Commandment. But the Talmud also records the rulings of rabbis who approved the use of figured mosaics and of rabbis who prayed in a synagogue containing a royal statue. The archaeological materials emphasize this variety.

Almost all aspects of Jewish life were deeply affected by the Graeco-Roman world which surrounded it. As one scholar has observed, "It is sufficient to state that no less than three thousand Greek words"—including synagogue, *archisynagogus* and *bema*—"are found throughout the early rabbinic literature to show how close those rabbis stood to Greek life."[22] According to a leading historian of the period, "The most orthodox Jews of Palestine were profoundly hellenized in the third century. Bar Kochba's letters in Greek show that the most rabid Jewish nationalists were no less hellenized."[23] Yet we may be sure that not all Jews would approve of Leda and the swan on their sarcophagus and not all rabbis would welcome a carved head of Medusa in their synagogue. Indeed, we must recognize, with Goodenough, that the rabbinic literature gives no hint of the widespread use of pagan symbols in synagogue art.[24]

The variation in attitude toward these pagan symbols is clear. But how do we explain the use of these pagan symbols by those Jews who did adopt them?

The explanation is multifold, for the reasons Jews adopted these pagan symbols varied. Sometimes the explanation was doubtless "mere decoration," just as the swastika in the Connecticut synagogue carried no symbolic meaning for the Connecticut Jews who originally put it there. It was simply a part of the design repertoire. In much the same way, Jews must have decorated their synagogues with rosettes, vines, shells (which Goodenough, incidentally, read as "a metaphor of the vulva"), wreaths and possibly even the cupids to hold them up, without any symbolic significance.

Other pagan myths might have become secularized, or so the Jews thought, just as Halloween and St. Valentine's Day and, to some extent, Christmas have become secularized in the United States today. Thus some pagan myths may have been thought to be mere stories without religious content. The vintners treading grapes in the Chorazim synagogue may be no more than this, and the Jewish worshippers may have found it less objectionable than a biblical scene which might in their minds trench too closely on the explicit prohibition of the Second Commandment against idolatry. With some sense it could be argued that a common laborer tramping grapes—even if it were part of a popular tale—was less likely to be adored in an objectionable way than, say, a portrait of Moses. For others, of course, biblical scenes were considered more appropriate to synagogue decoration, as at Beth Alpha and Jerash.

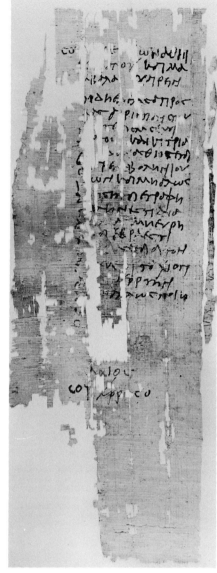

A letter from Bar-Kochba, written in Greek and recently found in a cave near the Dead Sea.

Chorazim—Vintners treading grapes in a Bacchic sequence.

159

A belief in magic and superstition has often existed side by side with more elevated religious beliefs, including those of Judaism.[25] This was surely true during the period of our ancient synagogues, and may in part account for these pagan symbols. Indeed, a belief in the influence of the planets on the affairs of the world was part of the intellectual baggage of the time. It permeated all religions and all peoples of the ancient world. To understand by comparison, one has only to consider the common belief, until perhaps the end of the last century, in the so-called evil eye. How often, even today, do we hear the Yiddish expression *"k'nein hora"* uttered in the face of something beautiful and good. A mother admiring her daughter says, "She is growing so fast, *k'nein hora.*" Literally, the phrase means "no evil eye" and is a formula intended to keep the evil eye from noticing the good or the beautiful which the speaker has just mentioned. Some third, fourth, and fifth-century Jews behaved similarly. They did not see a necessary conflict between traditional Judaism and a belief that by paying attention to the zodiac they might improve their chances of having sufficient rain at the right time. Indeed, even Rabbi Hanina declared it his opinion that the constellation under which a man is born determines his destiny.[26] The zodiac was a bit like the common man's insurance policy. If it didn't help, it wouldn't hurt.

The zodiac has been one of the more persistent elements in Jewish lore. Until modern times the prayer for rain on *Shemini Atzeret* was accompanied by a long *piyyut*, or religious poem, based on the twelve signs of the zodiac.[27] Not only was this *piyyut* printed in the *mahzor* or holiday prayer book, but a zodiac wheel was usually printed beside it. The zodiac was also a conspicuous motif on *Ketuboth*, or marriage contracts, of the seventeenth and eighteenth centuries. For these Jews and earlier ones who put zodiacs in their synagogues, there was no reason why their God could not work through the zodiac and reveal himself in this way. In short, traditional Jews found no difficulty in accepting a belief in the influence and importance of the zodiac's signs alongside their orthodox Jewish views. Perhaps a theologian or a logician could demonstrate a conflict between the zodiac and the more elevated beliefs of Judaism, but many other Jews, including some of their rabbis, did not perceive it. It was also probable that in many cases, the congregational laity were willing to accept more than their rabbinical leaders liked.

Sometimes pagan symbols were Judaized or given a Jewish content in the synagogue. For centuries, the calendar had been regarded as a reflection of godly regularity, and the zodiac may well have been a living symbol which many Jews adopted to represent this divine order. One scholar has suggested that in some instances the zodiac was divested of all idolatrous associations and, instead of standing for the heavenly constellations, it stood for the ordering of the Temple services throughout the year,[28] or for the Hebrew months, or the twelve tribes of Israel. In the zodiac in the Na'aran synagogue near Jericho, the personification of autumn carries a *shofar*. Another example of the Judaization of pagan themes comes from the Gaza synagogue mosaic in which King David is pictured as Orpheus playing his lute and taming wild beasts. What the Jews may really be saying is that our David has all the powers of Orpheus and more. Similarly at Dura-Europos, where Moses is portrayed carrying the club of Hercules; Jews attributed to Moses the accomplishments of Hercules.

Nor can we exclude the possibility that Helios in his chariot in the center of synagogue zodiacs represented an actual deity to whom some members of the congregation addressed prayers for practical purposes.[29] Some, in short, may have been idolators.

Thus, a wide variety of explanations accounts for the use of pagan symbols in ancient synagogues. And not all Jews or congregations were alike in their attitudes and understandings. The picture that emerges of Judaism is as rich, as varied, and with as many attachments to a majority culture as in our own day.

12 ✡ RECENT DISCOVERIES AT OSTIA AND SARDIS

Large urban synagogues in Italy and Turkey reflect a cosmpolitan Jewish world

At this point we are thoroughly familiar with the three major types of ancient synagogue architecture; the basilica-plan, the broadhouse-plan, and the apse-plan. (We have seen too that some synagogues, such as Ein-Gedi, don't fit any of the plans in our basic typology.) Now we shall consider two recently discovered and highly significant ancient synagogues which are in many ways unique, but which also have clear relationships to the plans in our basic typology.

The Jewish presence in ancient Rome has always been known and well-attested. From literary sources, from archaeological artifacts, from tombs, catacombs and inscriptions, we know that the Jews were a major Roman community. Yet, strangely enough, although at least eleven different synagogues and a host of synagogue officials are mentioned in Roman inscriptions, not a single ancient synagogue building has been found in Rome itself.[1]

That is one reason for the joy that greeted the discovery of the synagogue at Ostia in 1963. Ostia is only twelve miles from Rome and served as the port of the imperial city. Scholars knew that Jews must have lived in Ostia and participated in its commercial activity, yet until the 1960's, no evidence of a synagogue was found although major areas of ancient Ostia had long been excavated. When it was discovered, it was not found in the course of continuing archaeological excavation at Ostia, but rather by accident while building an expressway to Rome's new international airport, Leonardo da Vinci, at Fiumicino. Then the archaeologists were called in to excavate.

According to the excavators, a synagogue existed on this site at least from the first century C.E., although the latest synagogue, which has now been partially reconstructed, dates from the fourth century C.E. This building was abandoned about a century later as Ostia itself was declining and ultimately abandoned.

162

The Ostia synagogue has many interesting and several unique features. The synagogue room itself has three entrances, a large central one and two smaller ones on either side, as in the basilica-plan synagogues in the Galilee. Moreover, this entrance facade of the Ostia synagogue faces Jerusalem, just as do the basilica-plans. However, inside the synagogue is an imposing inner gateway formed by four columns of gray marble and white bases topped by Corinthian capitals. These four columns, arranged in a square, stand opposite the large center doorway of the entrance facade. On either side of the four-columned gateway, a wall extended to the side walls of the synagogue, thus requiring passage through the four-columned gateway to get to the prayer hall. As originally constructed, this fourth-century synagogue appears to have had no permanent Torah shrine as part of its structure. This demonstrates how late the tradition of the portable Torah shrine—with the worshippers turning around after they entered the prayer hall in order to face Jerusalem—persisted. The impressive four-columned inner gateway was probably intended as an inspiring entranceway for the mobile Torah shrine that was brought into the prayer room during the service.

This unusual, imposing architecture created special problems when the congregation, at a later stage in the building, decided to install a permanent Torah shrine. They could not simply close up the large central entrance door, as was done in basilica-plan synagogues, for in that case the Torah shrine would be behind the inner four-columned gateway—in another room, as it were, from the main sanctuary. Instead, one of the walls beside the inner gateway was torn down and in its place was constructed a free-standing apse-like *aedicula* with two free-standing columns connected to the ends of the apse by an architrave. This apse-like structure was approached by

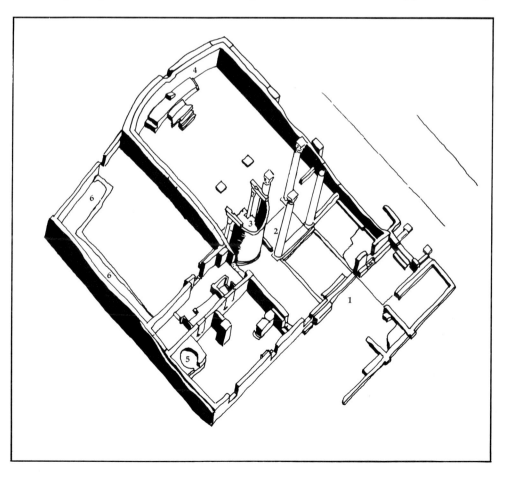

Ostia—A perspective drawing of the synagogue showing (1) the center door to the synagogue with smaller doors on either side, (2) inner, four-columned gateway, (3) apse-like Torah Shrine, (4) curved back wall, (5) oven, and (6) benches.

Ostia—The original Roman road leading to the synagogue in the background.

Ostia—The synagogue after partial excavation and before restoration.

Ostia—Two views of the four-columned gateway (the free-standing larger columns of gray marble with Corinthian capitals) and the Torah shrine on the right. The Torah shrine is apse-like and is approached by four steps. In front of the apse are two colonettes (small columns) surmounted by architraves connecting the colonettes to the apse.

four steps and into the apse was placed the Ark of the Law. This structure is unparalleled in synagogue architecture.

Another peculiarity of the Ostia synagogue is its slightly curving back wall, a feature also unique in ancient synagogue architecture. Set against this back wall is a puzzling kind of podium reached by a narrow set of steps. The excavator suggests that this podium was the *bema* from which the scriptural reading was given. But it seems strange to have this platform *behind* all the worshippers, especially when there was a perfectly obvious place for a *bema*—on the wall beside the inner four-columned gateway, to balance the Torah shrine on the opposite side. Perhaps this puzzling platform at the back of the prayer hall was a raised podium on which the elders or distinguished members of the community were seated. This suggestion receives some support, as we shall see, from the elders benches at the back of the Sardis synagogue. Or perhaps this podium at the back of the Ostia synagogue was a platform for a Torah shrine before the elaborate apse-like structure was built in the front part of the synagogue. Note that this podium on the back wall has a small raised structure in the center of it which could have supported a wooden Torah ark (a niche in the back wall may also have housed the Holy Scroll). Of course the difficulty with a Torah shrine placed on the back wall is that the worshippers would be facing away from Jerusalem when they faced the Torah shrine, but this may have been what eventually led to the major reconstruction in building the apse-like structure in the front of the prayer hall to house the Ark of the Law.

Adjacent to the synagogue are a number of rooms, two of which are quite spacious. In one of these was found a large oven, a table and a series of large jars sunk into the floor which could have stored wine, olive oil and other commodities. It has been suggested that the oven was used to bake the community's *matzah*, or unleavened bread, for the *Pesach* festival. But it was probably also used, along with the other facilities of the room, for various synagogue festivities. The room might also have served as a kitchen for those Jewish merchants and wayfarers who used the synagogue as a hostel. In this connection, the other large room attached to the synagogue is lined on two sides with unusually wide benches, which may have been used as beds. This room may also have served for meetings of the congregation and as the *beth ha-midrash* or schoolroom where the Law was taught.

All of these facilities adjacent to the synagogue bring to mind the inscription from a similar synagogue in Jerusalem in the days before the Roman destruction of the Temple, which we discussed many pages ago. Although we have not stopped to record the fact with respect to each synagogue we have discussed, many of these synagogues give evidence of having had adjacent communal facilities. The Ostia synagogue serves to emphasize that throughout the hundreds of years covered by our survey of ancient synagogues, the synagogue served not only as a house of prayer where the Jew spoke directly to his God, but also as a school for adults as well as children, a community center, and often as a hostel.

The floors of the Ostia synagogue were covered with mosaics, but unfortunately most are either in bad repair or destroyed. It appears that none of them contained a depiction of any living thing. Among the architectural fragments were a number of *menorot*, one of which appeared on part of the apse-like Torah shrine. In addition, the excavators found a shallow basin which was probably used for ablutions prior to prayer.

Sardis—This is the marble *menorah* plaque which helped identify the building as a synagogue. Were we not so familiar with the common combinations of Jewish symbols, we might have difficulty recognizing the *lulav* or palm branch to the left of the *menorah* and the *shofar* (shaped like a backward L) on the right. What are the curly lines beneath the branches of the *menorah* on either side of the stem? Answer: rolled up Torah scrolls viewed from the end.

Priene—A plaque from the synagogue. Two curly lines are seen beneath the branches of the *menorah*. These (and other examples like them) helped archaeologist Yigal Shiloh identify the curly lines in the Sardis *menorah* plaque (above right) as rolled up Torah scrolls. On the right of the *menorah* are a *lulav* and *shofar* which resemble the *lulav* and *shofar* of the Sardis plaque.

Perhaps the most unusual of the finds was an inscription dating from the late second or third century and which therefore belonged to one of the earlier synagogues on the same site. The inscription is in Greek and states that a certain Mindis Faustos arranged to have built and placed a container for the sacred Law. This was done "for the well-being of the Emperor"—these words alone (*pro salute Augusti*) are in Latin. No doubt this inscription refers to an earlier Ark of the Law. Was it a mobile one? Or a permanent one? Where was it placed? What did it look like? All of these questions must remain unanswered, for no trace of the ark has been found.[2]

The ancient synagogue of Sardis is different from all the other synagogues we have looked at in two respects: its size and its magnificence. It also reflects a different kind of Jewish community.

Located about 60 miles from the Aegean Sea in what is now Turkey but what in ancient times was Sardis, the capital of Lydia, this synagogue was discovered only in 1962, and the final publication of the excavation results has not yet appeared. Thus, much of what we say of this unusual building must be regarded as tentative. As this is being written, the excavators are also nearing completion of the restoration of the fourth-century synagogue. With much of its original magnificence intact, the Sardis synagogue promises to be a major stop for tourists in Turkey.

The discovery of the synagogue, in the fifth season of a joint Harvard-Cornell expedition to Sardis, came as somewhat of a shock to the excavators. Not that it would be so unusual to find a synagogue at Sardis; the surprise was that this particular building was a synagogue. The archaeologists were excavating what was as yet an unidentified, but obviously im-

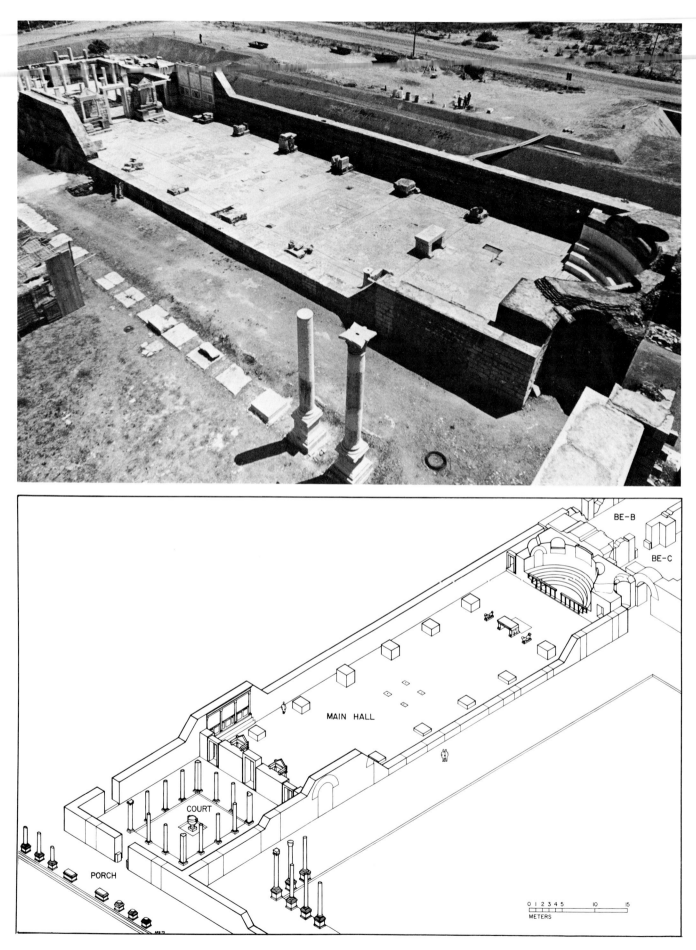

opposite
Sardis—An overview of the synagogue. All of the elements shown
in the drawing (below left) are
identifiable in this picture.
Note the niches from an earlier
phase of the building behind
the apse.

portant public building in the choicest location in town, right next to the
magnificent Marble Court, and behind the shops which lined the colonnade
known as Marble Avenue. Unexpectedly, they came upon some Hebrew
dedicatory inscriptions and a marble plaque with a *menorah* on it flanked
by a *lulav* and *shofar*. Another Hebrew inscription read "Peace unto
Israel," and the identification of the building as a synagogue became un-
mistakable.

A peculiar feature of the *menorah* on the marble plaque which helped to
identify the building as a synagogue are the little squiggly lines on either
side of the central stem of the *menorah*. The excavators attached no special
significance to them. But a piece of detective work by a Hebrew University
archaeologist, Yigal Shiloh, established that they are in fact the ends of
rolled up Torah scrolls.[3] This becomes evident when the picture of this
menorah is compared with other *menorah* representations from other
synagogues where the same rolled motif appears and where, taken all together, the identification is clear. Thus we add the Torah scroll to the list
of Jewish symbols which commonly appear together in synagogue art.

The Sardis building, whose final stage dates from the fourth century,
is entered through a splendid square colonnaded forecourt, in the center of
which was a huge marble crater with a vertically-fluted body and large
volute handles. Here the worshippers probably washed their hands before
prayer.

Leading the worshipper from the forecourt to the great basilical hall
were the customary three entrances, a large central one and a smaller one on
either side. Inside the entrance and on either side of the central portal was a
rectangular Torah shrine—although one only may have been a Torah
shrine and the other a *menorah* shrine, for purposes of symmetry. The
building was wide enough—60 feet—so that the two shrines for the Torah
and *menorah* could be installed *between* the entrances without blocking any
of the entrances themselves. The two shrines of course faced into the
prayer hall.

At the opposite end of the long and impressive prayer hall was a large
apse, entered by ascending steps and lined with three rows of semi-circular
benches. We have come to expect a Torah shrine in synagogue apses. But
that does not appear to have been the case at Sardis. The reason is obvious.
The apse at Sardis points west—in the opposite direction from Jerusalem.
As we shall explain in more detail later, the original apse was a survival
from an earlier stage of the building when it was probably not a synagogue. So the Jews added the benches and made it into a place of honor for
the Elders of the congregation. Some idea of the size of the building can be
gained from the fact that over 70 people can be comfortably accommodated
on the benches of the apse.

opposite
Sardis—A perspective drawing of
the synagogue. Reading from
right to left, we see the apse lined
with semi-circular benches, the
reading table flanked by crouching pairs of lions and a special
stone in front of the table where
the reader stood, the six piers
which extended from each of the
long walls creating bays, the
Torah shrine and *menorah* shrine
on either side of the center door,
the colonnaded forecourt with the
marble crater in the center, and
the entrance porch.

In front of the apse was an imposing marble table over seven feet long.
Instead of legs, it was supported at either end by an eagle in high relief,
with wings outspread and talons clutching a bundle of rods. These eagles
apparently date from a much earlier time—many hundreds of years—and
were reused by the Jews as table supports. Perhaps the bundles of rods
which the eagles grip in their talons were originally intended as the
thunderbolt of Zeus. In any event, the table which these eagles supported
was doubtless used for the reading of the Law. A marble pavement embedded in the floor on one side of the table indicates that the reader stood facing Jerusalem, not facing the Elders in the apse; perhaps the congregation
sat against the long walls facing into the center of the hall.

Flanking the reading table at either end were two pairs of free-standing lions almost life-size—one pair at each side—symbolically protecting the reading table with its sacred scroll. The lions—each pair crouching back to back—also appear to date from a much earlier time and were reused in the synagogue.

The long and inspiring prayer hall was not supported by columns but by six pairs of massive piers extending from the side walls, thus creating seven sections to the synagogue and seven pairs of bays. Each of these sections was paved with an intricate geometric mosaic and the walls were

Sardis—The Torah shrine and *menorah* shrine on either side of the center entrance to the synagogue.

Sardis—The reading table on which the Torah was placed. The eagle bases date from an earlier period and were reused in the synagogue.

172

finished with a marble revetment and painted reliefs, fragments of which reveal at least a half-dozen kinds of colored marble. The synagogue—390 feet long from end to end—could accommodate over a thousand people, not including the gallery which may have been for women. The overall effect must have been awe-inspiring. The size and proportion of the room were mighty and the furnishings and decorations luxurious. The combination resulted in an interior of extraordinary splendor. Indeed, the excavators have suggested that the impression it gave was "not unlike the great decorative schemes ... seen later in monuments like San Vitale and Hagia Sophia."[4]

In an earlier stage of the synagogue—in the third century—there was no

Sardis—The colonnaded forecourt with a large fluted crater in the center. Note the heart-shaped corner columns similar to those found in basilica-plan synagogues in the Galilee.

173

forecourt and no Torah or *menorah* shrines on the inside of the entrance facade. These were added in a fourth century reconstruction. Prior to this remodeling, the Sardis congregation apparently used a portable Torah shrine which was brought into the giant building through the center of the three doors, just as it was brought into the little basilica-plan synagogues of the Galilee. However, even in this third-century phase, the synagogue had its bench-lined apse for the elders.

More interesting than this third-century phase is a previous phase when the building in all probability was not used as a synagogue. Its special interest derives from the fact that it tells us a great deal about the Jewish community of Sardis. In its pre-synagogue phase the building was basically the same except that the apse, instead of being lined with benches, had three niches in it. These could well have been for images of the emperor or divinities. The plan of the building—very long and comparatively narrow—suggests that it was originally constructed as a Roman civil basilica. The function of the building, the excavators speculate, was a judicial tribunal. The location, as well as the building itself, would appear to be ideal for this purpose. Convenient to the gymnasium—indeed in an even earlier stage gymnasium buildings, perhaps dressing rooms, were on this site—adjacent to the city's magnificent Marble Court, immediately behind the shops on Sardis' main street which itself was 50 feet wide and paved with marble, the civil basilica formed the focus of a thriving bazaar area.

The difficult question is, how did this magnificent building with its unparalleled location happen to be sold or otherwise transferred to the Jewish community for its synagogue, especially if it had been used as a judicial tribunal? No detailed answer to this question can be given. But in general the answer appears to relate to the unusual influence and prosperity of the Jewish community of Sardis. (Incidentally, the fact that the many donors' inscriptions in the synagogue seem to deal only with the interior decoration and furnishings is consistent with the fact that the Jewish community acquired the building after it had already been constructed.) The prosperity of the Jewish community is clearly reflected in the many shops near the synagogue which were apparently owned by Jewish merchants, as indicated by the Jewish names scratched on jars found in these shops. That this may have become a Jewish commercial area may also have played a part in the transfer of the building to the Jewish community for use as a synagogue. Several of the synagogue inscriptions refer to the donors as goldsmiths and jewellers, and their shops too may have adjoined the synagogue. The communal standing of the members of the congregation is reflected in other synagogue inscriptions in which one man is referred to as "citizen of Sardis"; others are described as city councilors, record-office functionaries in the Roman provincial administration and a former procurator. What emerges is a picture of a highly hellenized Jewish community, prosperous and influential, active in civic and communal affairs.

The Sardis synagogue is unique because it reflects a large, prosperous, urban Jewish community. None of the other ancient synagogues we have examined even approach the scale of the Sardis synagogue and most of them belonged to small, rural communities far from the centers of commerce and culture. Much of the art from this cultural hinterland can almost be described as folk art, deriving its power and attraction principally from its simplicity and naivete. But when Jews lived in cultural centers, as we know they did—even though the Sardis synagogue is the only surviving synagogue building from such a center—the grandeur of their buildings rivalled the best of the age. As we have already noted, the excavators have compared the decorative scheme of the Sardis synagogue to San Vitale and Hagia Sophia. Elsewhere they describe the sculpture which was built into the walls and piers of the synagogue as being of the "finest quality" even though only fragments remain;[5] and a marble *menorah* is described as "technically . . . a virtuoso piece."[6] If Sardis is any guide, the best of Jewish art favorably compared with the best of the art of the larger community of its time. Unfortunately, most of this Jewish art has not survived. And the remains of Sardis are only an apercu of vanished splendors.[7]

NOTES

Chapter 1
The Story of Ancient Synagogues

1. George Foot Moore in his classic study, *Judaism In the First Centuries of the Christian Era*, Volume I (Cambridge, 1927), p. 284, called the synagogue "a wholly unique institution."
2. Michael Avi-Yonah, "Synagogue Architecture In the Late Classical Period," *Jewish Art*, C. Roth (ed.), pp. 65-82 (Connecticut, 1971), p. 82.
3. Floyd V. Filson, "Part IV—Temple, Synagogue and Church," *The Biblical Archaeologist*, Volume VII, pp. 77-88 (December, 1944), p. 79.
4. See, e.g., Floyd V. Filson, "Part IV—Temple, Synagogue and Chruch," *The Biblical Archaeologist*, Volume VII, pp. 77-88 (December, 1944), p. 88; H. G. May, "Synagogues In Palestine," *The Biblical Archaeologist*, Volume VII, pp. 1-20 (February, 1944), p. 20; J. W. Crowfoot, *Early Churches In Palestine* (London, 1941), pp. 159-160; E. L. Sukenik, *Ancient Synagogues In Palestine and Greece* (London, 1934), p. 2; "Synagogue," *Encyclopedia Judaica*, Volume XV, pp. 579-629 (Jerusalem, 1971), p. 579; M. Avi-Yonah, "Synagogue Architecture In the Late Classical Period," *Jewish Art*, C. Roth (ed.), pp. 65-82 (Connecticut, 1971), p. 66.
5. George Foot Moore, *Judaism In the First Centuries of the Christian Era*, Volume I (Cambridge, 1927), p. 285. See Franz Landsberger, "The Sacred Direction or Synagogue and Church, *Hebrew Union College Annual*, Volume XXVIII, pp. 181-203 (Cincinnati, 1957), p. 188 (Reprinted in *The Synagogue: Studies In Origins, Archaeology and Architecture*, J. Gutmann (ed.), pp. 239-261 (New York, 1975), p. 246.

6. For detailed references to the activities described in this paragraph, see Lee I. Levine, "Roman Caesarea, An Archaeological-Topographical Study", *Qedem*, Monographs of the Institute of Archaeology, The Hebrew University, Vol. II (1975), pp. 41-45.
7. Salo Baron, *A Social and Religious History of the Jews*, Volume II (New York, 1952), pp. 285, 291.

Chapter 2
Synagogues Before the Roman Destruction of the Temple

1. Yigael Yadin, *Masada* (New York, 1966), p. 184.
2. However, since then, in 1966, a similar synagogue was excavated at Herodium. V.C. Corbo, "L'Herodion di Giabal Fureidis," *Studii Biblici Franciscani Liber Annuus*, Volume XVII, pp. 5-121 (Jerusalem, 1967), pp. 101-103; V.C. Corbo, "The Excavations of Herodium," *Qadmoniot*, Volume I, No. 4 (Jerusalem, 1968), pp. 132-136 (Hebrew); See below, p. 29.
3. Professor Yadin also qualifies his statement by limiting it to Israel.
4. *Ketuboth* 105a. Elsewhere the figure 480 is given. *Talmud Yerushalmi Megillah* III:1. It may be that this latter figure is intended as an approximate figure, like the use of 40 years in the Bible as an indication of a generation, of which 480 is a multiple.
5. See S.J. Saller, *Second Revised Catalog of the Ancient Synagogues of the Holy Land* (Jerusalem, 1972), p. 13.
6. Salo Baron, *A Social and Religious History of the Jews*, Volume I (New York, 1952), p. 277.

7. Lee Levine, "Roman Caesarea, An Archaeological-Topographical Study," *Qedem*, Volume II (Jerusalem, 1975), pp. 42-43.

8. *Mishnah, Yoma* VII:1; *Tosephta Sukkah* IV:5; *Sukkah* 54a; but see S.B. Hoenig, "The Supposititious Temple-Synagogue", *Jewish Quarterly Review*, Volume 54, pp. 115-131 (1963) (Reprinted in *The Synagogue: Studies in Origins, Archaeology and Architecture*, J. Gutmann (ed.) (New York, 1975), pp. 55-71.

9. III Maccabees 7:20. This citation speaks of the dedication of a "place of prayer."

10. J.B. Frey, *Corpus Inscriptionum Judicarum*, Volume II (Rome, 1952), p. 367. The word used for synagogue is *proseuche* (prayerhouse), which was the word used for synagogue by the community of Egypt at the time. Even in Philo and Josephus *proseuche* predominates over "synagogue" for Jewish houses of worship. While most scholars accept *proseuche* as the equivalent of synagogue (See Martin Hengel, "Proseuche und Synagoge: Judische Gemeinde, Gotteshaus und Gottesdienst In der Diaspora und In Palastina," *Tradition und Glaube. Das Fruhe Chritentum in seiner Umwelt. Festgabe fur Karl Georg Kuhn zum 65*, Gert Jeremias *et. al.* (eds.) (Gottingen, 1971), pp. 157-183 (Reprinted in *The Synagogue: Studies In Origins, Archaeology and Architecture*, J. Gutmann (ed.) (New York, 1975), pp. 27-54), others do not. (See E. Rivkin, "Ben Sira and the Non-Existence of the Synagogue: A Study In Historical Method," *In the Time of Harvest. Essays In Honor of Abba Hillel Silver.* D.J. Silver (ed.), pp. 320-354 (New York, 1963), pp. 331-334; G.M. Barlink, "Maison de prieré comme denomination de l'eglise en tant qu'-edifice, en particular chez Eusebe de Cesaree," *Revues des Etudes Greques*, Volume LXXXIV (Paris, 1971), pp. 101-118); J. Gutmann "The Origin of the Synagogue" *Archaeologischer Anzeiger=Beiblatt zum Jahrbruch des Deutschen Archaeologischen Instituts*, 87/1 (1972), pp. 36-40 (Reprinted in *The Synagogue: Studies in Origins, Archaeology and Architecture*, J. Gutmann (ed.) New York, (1975), pp. 72-76. *Proseuche* can also mean prayer, as in the Delos Inscription. See below p. 44.

11. The possibility that a synagogue in Palestine is mentioned on a 6th century ostracon should also be noted (C.C. Torrey, "A Synagogue At Elath?" *Bulletin of the American Schools of Oriental Research*, No. 84 (December, 1941), pp. 4-5), but this reading is, as Torrey recognizes, not only "unexpected," but "startling." The reading of this ostracon by the excavator, Nelson Glueck, is far more likely. Nelson Glueck, "Ostraca From Elath," *Bulletin of the American Schools of Oriental Research*, No. 82, pp. 3-11 (April, 1941), pp. 9-11. Other pre-destruction synagogue inscriptions may be found in J.B. Frey, *Corpus Inscriptionum Judicarum*, Volume II (Rome, 1952), Nos. 1441-1442 (dated to between 143-116 B.C.E.) and No. 1449 (dated by one authority to about 35 B.C.E.).

12. See, for example, Louis Finkelstein, "The Origin of the Synagogue," *Proceedings of the American Academy for Jewish Research, 1928-1930*, pp. 49-59 (Philadelphia, 1930), p. 49 (Reprinted in *The Synagogue: Studies In Origins, Archaeology and Architecture*, J. Gutmann (ed.), pp. 3-13 (New York, 1975), p. 3); J. Morgenstern, "The Origin of the Synagogue," *Studi Orientalistici In Onore di Giorgio Levi Della Vidi*, Giovanni Bardi (ed.), Volume II, pp. 192-201 (Rome, 1956), p. 192; but compare S. Zeitlin, "The Origin of the Synagogue: A Study In the Development of Jewish Institutions," *Proceedings of the American Academy of Jewish Research, 1930-1931* (Philadelphia, 1931), pp. 69-81 (Reprinted in *The Synagogue: Studies In Origins, Archaeology and Architecture*, J. Gutmann (ed.) (New York, 1975), pp. 14-26).

13. See, e.g., Mitchell Dahood, *The Anchor Bible-Psalms 51-100* (New York, 1968), p. 199. A Maccabean date is now ruled out for this psalm by psalms found among the Dead Sea Scrolls. However, a date shortly after 485 B.C.E. is still possible.

14. See Roland de Vaux, *Ancient Israel*, Volume II (paperback ed., New York, 1965), p. 343; H.G. May, "Synagogues In Palestine," *The Biblical Archaeologist*, Volume VII, pp. 1-20 (February, 1944), p. 2. See, generally, I. Sonne, "Synagogue," *The Interpreter's Dictionary of the Bible*, Volume IV (New York, 1962), pp. 476-491.

15. Architectural fragments of a building which may have been part of a pre-destruction synagogue have been found at Jerash, now in Jordan. A.H. Detweiler, "Some Early Jewish Architectural Vestiges From Jerash," *Bulletin of the American Schools of Oriental Research*, No. 87, (October, 1942), pp. 10-17.

16. Whether it was in fact the Zealots or others who defended Masada and who the Zealots and Sicarii were is a matter of considerable debate. The materials are collected in Morton Smith, "Zealots and Sicarii, Their Origin and Relation," *Harvard Theological Review*, Volume CXIV (Cambridge, 1941), pp. 1-19.

17. At one time, Yadin suggested that this room might be the dwelling of the person responsible for the maintenance of the building. Y. Yadin, "The Excavation of Masada 1963/1964 Preliminary Report," *Israel Exploration Journal*, Volume XV, pp. 1-120 (1965), p. 78.

18. Gideon Foerster, "The Synagogues at Masada and Herodium," *Eretz Israel*, Volume XI (1975), pp. 224-228 (Hebrew; summary in English, p. 30). *Cf.*, Franz Landsberger, "The Sacred Direction In Synagogue and Church," *Hebrew Union College Annual*, Volume XXVIII (1957), pp. 181-203 (Reprinted in *The Synagogue: Studies In Origins, Archaeology and Architecture*. J. Gutmann (ed.) (New York, 1975), pp. 239-261).

19. *Tosephta Megillah* IV:22.

20. See, for example, the first four *Mishnaot* in *Rosh Hashanah*.

21. See S.J. Saller, *Second Revised Catalog of the Ancient Synagogues of the Holy Land* (Jerusalem, 1972), p. 41.

Chapter 3
Discovering Ancient Synagogues

1. S.J. Saller, *Second Revised Catalogue of the Ancient Synagogues of the Holy Land* (Jerusalem, 1972).

2. *Tosephta Sukkah* IV. The *hazzan* was one of the principal synagogue functionaries but at this period, he had not yet adopted the regular duty of serving as a cantor, which is what a modern *hazzan* does.

3. L.H. Vincent, "Vestiges d'une Synagogue Antique a Yafa de Galilee," *Revue Biblique*, Volume XXX, pp. 434-443 (1921), p. 436. The synagogue from which this lintel apparently came was later excavated by E.L. Sukenik. See E.L. Sukenik, "The Ancient Synagogue At Yafa Near Nazareth," *Louis M. Rabinowitz Fund for the Exploration of Ancient Synagogues, Bulletin II* (1951), pp. 6-24. However, as E.R. Goodenough points out, the relationship of the lintel to the excavated building has not been made clear. E.R. Goodenough, *Jewish Symbols In the Greco-Roman Period*, Volume XII (New York, 1965), p. 45.

4. This mosque was originally a crusader church.

5. J. Prawer, *The Latin Kingdom of Jerusalem* (London, 1972), p. 300.

6. This story is told in Joan Comay, *An Uncommon Guide* (New York, 1969), p. 143.

7. J.W. Crowfoot and R.W. Hamilton, "The Discovery of a Synagogue At Jerash," *Palestine Exploration Fund Quarterly Statement*, Volume IX, pp. 211-219 (1929). p. 211.

8. J.W. Crowfoot and R.W. Hamilton, "The Discovery of a Synagogue At Jerash," *Palestine Exploration Fund Quarterly Statement*, Volume IX, pp. 211-219 (1929). p. 211

9. See Lee I. Levine, "Roman Caesarea, An Archaeological-Topographical Study," *Qedem*, Monographs of the Institute of Archaeology, The Hebrew University, Vol. II (1975), p. 26, n. 176.

10. S.J. Saller, *Second Revised Catalogue of the Ancient Synagogues of the Holy Land* (Jerusalem, 1972), pp. 79-80.

11. See H. Kjaer, "The Excavations of Shilo (1929), *Palestine Oriental Society Journal*, Volume X, Nos. 2-3, pp. 87-174 (1930), p. 167; See also S.J. Saller, *Second Revised Catalogue of the Ancient Synagogues of the Holy Land* (Jerusalem, 1972), pp. 79-80.

12. Whether and to what extent Judaeo-Christians lived in Palestine during the pre-Constantine period has recently been the subject of much investigation. See I. Mancini, *Archaeological Discoveries Relative to the Judeo-Christians* (Jerusalem, 1970).

13. See M. Avi-Yonah, "Synagogue Architecture In the Late Classical Period," *Jewish Art*, C. Roth (ed.), pp. 65-82 (Connecticut, 1971), p. 67. Rachel Wischnitzer, *The Architecture of the European Synagogue* (Philadelphia, 1964), p. 11. Several scholars, however, regard the question as still open. See, e.g., E.R. Goodenough, *Jewish Symbols In the Greco-Roman Period*, Volume II (New York, 1953), pp. 72-75. Goodenough's treatment of the Delos synagogue is criticized in M. Avi-Yonah, "Review," *Israel Exploration Journal*, Volume VI, No. 3 (1956), pp. 194-199. Strangely enough, Avi-Yonah himself refers to the Delos remains as a synagogue in "Synagogue—Architecture," *Encyclopedia Judaica*, Volume XV, pp. 595-600 (Jerusalem, 1971), p. 599. L.I. Rabinowitz, whether advisedly or because he was unaware that Sukenik reversed himself with respect to the Delos remains, relies on Sukenik's earlier statement and refers to the Delos remains as a synagogue in "Synagogue—Origins and History," *Encyclopedia Judaica*, Volume XV, pp. 579-584 (Jerusalem, 1971), p. 582; See also, P. Bruneau, *Recherches sur les cultes de Delos a l'epoque hellenistique et a l'epoque imperiale* (Paris, 1970), pp. 480-493, who takes strong issue with Mazur, although Bruneau is apparently unaware of Sukenik's change of position and all the reasons for it, such as the lead on top of the votive columns which probably was used to attach a figure to the columns.

14. E.L. Sukenik, *Ancient Synagogues In Palestine and Greece* (London, 1934), p. 38.

15. E.L. Sukenik, "The Present State of Ancient Synagogue Studies," *Louis M. Rabinowitz Fund for the Exploration Of Ancient Synagogues, Bulletin I*, pp. 8-23 (1949), pp. 21-22.

16. Belle D. Mazur, *Studies On Jewry In Greece*, Volume I (Athens, 1935), pp. 15-24.

17. A. Plassart, *Melanges Holleaux, Recueil de Memoires Concernant l'antique Grecque* (Paris, 1913), p. 211.

18. T. Wiegand and M. Schrader, *Priene, Ergebaisse der Ausgrabungen* (Berlin, 1904), p. 480.

19. E.L. Sukenik, *Ancient Synagogues In Palestine and Greece* (London, 1934), p. 43.

20. Rachel Wischnitzer, *The Architecture of the European Synagogue* (Philadelphia, 1954), p. 12, collects the arguments and arrives at the conclusion I have adopted. M. Avi-Yonah, "Synagogue Architecture In the Late Classical Period," *Jewish Art*, C. Roth (ed.), pp. 65-82 (Connecticut, 1971), p. 81, however, strongly doubts the building was ever a synagogue. But compare Don A. Halperin, *The Ancient Synagogues of the Iberian Peninsula* (University of Florida, Gainesville, 1969), pp. 25-27, who identifies not only the building at Elche as a synagogue, but also some ruins at Sadaba, Sargossa.

21. M. Avi-Yonah, "The Mosaics of Mopsuestia—Church or Synagogue?" *Qadmoniot*, Volume V, No. 2 (1972), pp. 62-65 (Hebrew).

22. J. Pinkerfeld "'David's Tomb'—Notes on the History of a Building", *Bulletin of the Louis M. Rabinowitz Fund for the Exploration of Ancient Synagogues, Bulletin III*, pp. 41-43 (December 1960).

23. Some scholars believe that this synagogue was a Judaeo-Christian synagogue. See B. Bagatti, *Saint Jacques le Mineur* (Edition "La Terre Sainte," Jerusalem 1962), pp. 14-21 ("Sainte Sion").

Chapter 4
Styles of Synagogue Architecture

1. However, there may be a first century C.E. synagogue beneath the recently excavated synagogue at Stobi, Yugoslavia. In 1972, flagstone paving which may have belonged to this early synagogue was found beneath the third and fourth century synagogues built on top of it. James Wiseman, *Stobi, A Guide to the Excavations* (Belgrad, 1973), p. 33.

2. Code of Theodosius XVI 8:25 and 8:27 (*The Theodosian Code*, Clyde Pharr (trans.) (Princeton, 1952), pp. 47-471).

3. As Isaiah Sonne has written, "The search for a line of development of synagogue architecture which would enable us to assign to each of the discovered types its proper place and date is still at the stage of mere speculation," *The Interpreter's Dictionary of the Bible*, Volume IV, pp. 476-491 (New York, 1962), p. 485. See also E.R. Goodenough, *Jewish Symbols In the Greco-Roman Period*, Volume I (New York, 1953), pp. 226-227; E.M. Meyers, "Synagogue, Architecture", *The Interpreter's Dictionary of the Bible, Supplement*, pp. 842-844 (Nashville 1976).

4. I Kings 8:30. See also Daniel 6:10, which is likewise used as a basis for synagogue orientation.

5. See *Tosephta Berakoth 3*.

6. The orientation toward Jerusalem is often only approximate and often depends on the site.

7. *Mishnah Ta'anith* 2:1; *Ta'anith* 15a; *Tosephta Megillah* 4:21; *Sotah* 39b. However, as Dr. Lee Levine has pointed out to me, all these references are to fast days when prayers were held in the city square. This does not necessarily indicate what was done at other times. See S. Krauss, *Synagogale Altertüemer* (Berlin, 1922), p. 324; but *cf.* Franz Landsberger, "The Sacred Direction In Synagogue and Church," *Hebrew Union College Annual*, Volume XXVIII, pp. 181-203 (1957), p. 184 (Reprinted in *The Synagogue: Studies In Origins, Archaeology and Architecture*, J. Gutmann (ed.), pp. 239-261 (New York, 1975), p. 242. Rabbi Louis Ginzberg has suggested another reason for the change in synagogue orientation: "Public prayer," he says, "originally meant recital of prayers by the reader, and hence his orientation was all important. As he had to face the congregation—this rule is often mentioned—it was considered desirable to have the people enter from the south side (in Galilean synagogues) so that the reader faced them and at the same time the Holy City. Later, however, with the increasing knowledge of Hebrew, the language of prayer, public prayer among the Galileans consisted of simultaneous prayer by the congregation. Consequently though the reader would repeat the main prayers . . . for the benefit 'of the ignorant,' it was of course the orientation of the congregation toward the Holy City that was of importance. The entrance was therefore transferred from the south to the north side (in synagogues north of Jerusalem)." Louis Ginzberg, *A Commentary On the Palestinian Talmud* (New York, 1941), pp. lxx-lxxi.

8. *Shabbath* 72b.

Chapter 5
Basilica-Plan Synagogues

1. E.L. Sukenik, *Ancient Synagogues In Palestine and Greece* (London, 1934), p. 47; E.L. Sukenik, "The Ancient Synagogue of El-Hammeh," *Journal of the Palestine Oriental Society*, Volume XV, pp. 101-180 (1935), pp. 162-163; Salo Baron, *A Social and Religious History of the Jews*, Volume II (New York, 1952), pp. 240-241. See also Zechariah 12:12-14 for supposed biblical support for the custom of separating the sexes.

2. Shmuel Safrai, "Was There A Women's Gallery In the Synagogue of Antiquity?" *Tarbiz*, Volume XXXII, No. 4 (1963), pp. 329-338 (Hebrew; summary in English, p. II).

2a. Recent excavations suggest that this installation or *aedicula* may well have been on either side of the main entrance, without blocking it, similar to the two shrines on either side of the main entrance in the Sardis synagogue described in Chapter XII. See J. F. Strange, "The Capernaum and Herodium Publications", *Bulletin of the American Schools of Oriental Research*, No. 226 (April 1977), pp. 65-73, p. 70.

3. Only at a later period does the *menorah* become a really common and conspicuous item of synagogue decoration. The problem during this earlier period may have been a ruling, later codified in the Talmud, prohibiting the making of a *menorah* like that in the Temple. See below, p. 110.

4. Gershom Scholem, "Magen David," *Encyclopedia Judaica*, Volume XI, pp. 687-697 (Jerusalem, 1971), p. 696; Gershom Scholem, *The Messianic Idea In Judaism* (New York, 1971), pp. 257-281.

5. G. Orfali, *Capharnaum et Ses Ruines* (Paris, 1922), pp. 67-86.

6. E.L. Sukenik, *Ancient Synagogues In Palestine and Greece* (London, 1934), p. 68.

7. Gideon Foerster, *Galilean Synagogues and Their Relation to Hellenistic and Roman Art and Architecture* (Ph.D. Thesis, Hebrew University, 1972), p. II (Hebrew; summary in English).

8. *Ibid.*; see also H.G. May, "Synagogues In Palestine," *The Biblical Archaeologist*, Volume VII, No. 1, pp. 1-20 (February, 1944), p. 5.

9. M. Avi-Yonah, "Editor's Note," *Israel Exploration Journal*, Volume XXIII, No. 1, pp. 43-45 (1973), p. 43. Isaiah Sonne also suggests that the synagogue in which Jesus preached probably stood on this spot. I. Sonne, "Synagogue," *The Interpreter's Dictionary of the Bible*, Volume IV, pp. 476-491 (New York, 1962), p. 481.

10. S. Loffreda, "The Late Chronology of the Synagogue at Capernaum," *Israel Exploration Journal*, Volume XXIII, No. 1, pp. 37-42 (1973), p. 37.

11. See G. Foerster, "The Recent Excavations at Capernaum," *Qadmoniot*, Volume IV, No. 1 (1971), pp. 126-131 (Hebrew); G. Foerster, "Notes On Recent Excavations at Capernaum (Review Article)," *Israel Exploration Journal*, Volume XXI, No. 4, pp. 207-211 (1971), p. 207.

12. M. Avi-Yonah, "Editor's Note," *Israel Exploration Journal*, Volume XXIII, No. 1, pp. 43-45 (1973), p. 45.

13. *Ibid.*

14. S. Loffreda, "The Late Chronology of the Synagogue at Capernaum," *Israel Exploration Journal*, Volume XXIII, No. 1, pp. 37-42 (1973), p. 40.

15. M. Avi-Yonah, "Editor's Note," *Israel Exploration Journal*, Volume XXIII, No. 1, pp. 42-45 (1973), p. 43; G. Foerster, "Notes On Recent Excavations at Capernaum," *Israel Exploration Journal*, Volume XXI, No. 4, pp. 207-211 (1971), pp. 208-209.

16. S. Loffreda, "The Late Chronology of the Synagogue at Capernaum," *Israel Exploration Journal*, Volume XXIII, No. 1, pp. 37-42 (1973), p. 40.

17. M. Avi-Yonah, "Editor's Note," *Israel Exploration Journal*, Volume XXIII, No. 1, pp. 43-45 (1973), p. 43. That there are so many coins at Capernaum—obviously purposely placed, not lost, beneath the floor—suggests that they were put there not when the building was built, but sometime later, when danger threatened, in the vain hope of hiding them and returning later to reclaim them.

18. Capernaum is among the larger basilica-plan synagogues. This emphasizes how small almost all of these ancient synagogues were, with the notable exception of Sardis. See Chapter XII.

19. Scholars are in dispute as to whether iconoclasts or the ravages of time were responsible for the disappearance of many of the carved figures at Chorazim. See E.R. Goodenough, *Jewish Symbols In the Greco-Roman Period*, Volume I (New York, 1953), p. 193.

Chapter 6
Dura-Europos

1. A dedicatory inscription on the ceiling of the synagogue to be described contains a date which corresponds to 245 C.E., so we may accept that as the date of the completion of the building. The paintings were probably added thereafter and took several years to complete. C.H. Kraeling, *The Synagogue, Excavations at Dura-Europos, Final Report VIII*, Volume I (New Haven, 1956), p. 333. Rostovtzeff notes some dipinti in the synagogue are dated 256 C.E., so the synagogue could not have been destroyed before this date. M. Rostovtzeff, *Dura-Europos and Its Art* (Oxford, 1938), p. 29. While Kraeling gives the date of its destruction as "ca. 256 C.E." (p. 4), Rostovtzeff suggests that the city was destroyed somewhat later "in one of the great raids of Shapur into Syria which culminated in the capture of Antioch between 258 and 260 C.E." (p. 29). An extended discussion regarding the date of the destruction of Dura-Europos may be found in Rostovtzeff, "Res Gestae Divi Saporis and Dura," *Berytus*, Volume VIII, pp. 17-60 (1943), pp. 48-60; A. Bellinger, "The Numismatic Evidence From Dura," *Berytus*, Volume VIII (1943), pp. 61-71.

2. A small Christian community also lived in Dura-Europos as indicated by a church which has been excavated, as well as a large number of adherents of Mithraism.

3. Shmuel Safrai, "Was There A Women's Gallery In the Synagogue of Antiquity?" *Tarbiz*, Volume XXXII, No. 4 (1963), pp. 329-338 (Hebrew; summary in English, p. II) disputes the excavators' conclusion that there was a separate women's section in the Dura-Europos synagogue.

3a. Clark Hopkins, "The Excavations of the Dura Synagogue Paintings," in *The Dura-Europos Synagogue: A Re-Evaluation* (1932-1972), J. Gutmann, ed. (American Academy of Religion and Society of Biblical Literature 1973), pp. 10-21, p. 16.

4. This account has been taken largely from C.H. Kraeling, *The Synagogue, Excavations at Dura-Europos, Final Report VIII*, Volume I (New Haven, 1956), pp. 385-402 and M. Rostovtzeff, *Dura-Europos and Its Art* (Oxford, 1938), pp. 1-4.

5. Esther 2:21-23; 6:1-11.

6. E.R. Goodenough, *Jewish Symbols In the Greco-Roman Period*, Volume IX (New York, 1964), p. 181.

7. See M. Avi-Yonah, Book Review, *Journal of the Palestine Oriental Society*, Volume XXI (1948), pp. 177-181; C.H. Kraeling, *The Synagogue, Excavations at Dura-Europos, Final Report VIII*, Volume I (New Haven, 1956), pp. 89-90, 352; but see E.R. Goodenough, *Jewish Symbols In the Greco-Roman Period*, Volume X (New York, 1964), pp. 100-104.

8. See S.M. Paul "Jerusalem—A City of Gold." *Israel Exploration Journal*, Volume XVII, (1967), pp. 259-63; H.A. Hoffner Jr., "The 'City of Gold' and the 'City of Silver,'" *Israel Exploration Journal*, Volume XIX, (1969), pp. 178-80; and letter to the editor by Jane Cooper, *Israel Exploration Journal*, Volume XXV, (1975), pp. 191-192.

9. Many scholars believe that early Christian art was based on earlier Jewish art. Kurt Weitzmann of Princeton University has recently written:

   When Christians began to create pictorial art based to a large extent on representations of Biblical stories, Old Testament scenes, especially at first, played a much greater role than New Testament scenes and continued to be prominent. The reason for this became apparent in 1932 after Yale University excavated in the synagogue of Dura Europos in Syria, which is datable to the middle of the third century after Christ. Its wall paintings displayed an extraordinary repertory of scenes from various books of the Old Testament. This suggests that the Christians were not the first to illustrate the Bible, but relied on fully developed Jewish models. ("Late Antique and Early Christian Art", *Archaeology*, Volume XXX, pp. 412-417, pp.

414-415 (1977)).
See also J. Gutmann, "Are the Origins of Christian Art Jewish?", *Perspectives in Jewish Learning*, Volume V, pp. 41-47 (1973).

10. E.R. Goodenough, *Jewish Symbols In the Greco-Roman Period*, Volume IX (New York, 1964), p. 200.

Chapter 7
Broadhouse-Plan Synagogues

1. See, e.g., M. Avi-Yonah, "Synagogue Architecture In the Late Classical Period," *Jewish Art*, C. Roth (ed.), pp. 65-82 (Connecticut, 1971), pp. 71-80; M. Avi-Yonah, "Synagogue-Architecture," *Encyclopedia Judaica*, Volume XV, pp. 595-600 (Jerusalem, 1971), p. 598.

2. Michael Avi-Yonah, "Ancient Synagogues," *Ariel*, No. 32, pp. 29-43 (Jerusalem, 1973), p. 41.

3. See Erwin R. Goodenough, *Jewish Symbols In the Greco-Roman Period*, Volume IX, (New York, 1964), p. 15.

4. See Eric M. Meyers, A.T. Kraabel and James Strange, "Archaeology and Rabbinic Tradition at Khirbet Shema, 1970 and 1971 Campaigns," *The Biblical Archaeologist*, Volume XXXV, pp. 2-31 (February, 1972), p. 10; Eric M. Meyers, "The Ancient Synagogue of Khirbet Shema," *Perspectives In Jewish Learning*, Volume V, pp. 28-40 (1973), p. 30.

5. But note E.R. Goodenough's suggestion that the Dura niche was too small to be used for a permanent house for the Torah scroll. E.R. Goodenough, *Jewish Symbols In the Greco-Roman Period*, Volume XII (New York, 1965), p. 160.

Chapter 8
Apse-Plan Synagogues

1. E.R. Goodenough believes that the Dura-Europos niche was not a permanent house for the Torah. E.R. Goodenough, *Jewish Symbols In the Greco-Roman Period*, Volume XII (New York, 1965), p. 160.

2. This description may be compared with R. Hachlili, "The Niche and the Ark in Ancient Synagogues," *Bulletin of the American Schools of Oriental Research*, No. 223 (October, 1976), pp. 43-53.

3. I. Sonne, "Synagogue," *The Interpreter's Dictionary of the Bible*, Volume IV, pp. 476-491 (New York, 1962), pp. 487-488. See *Shabbath* 32a, declaring it to be a sin punishable by death to call the Holy Ark a chest. For an interesting misunderstanding of this passage, see Franz Landsberger, *A History of Jewish Art* (Cincinnati, 1946), p. 147: "Originally it was a chest, but in later times when it had become a sacred Ark, no one wanted to be reminded of its secular origin."

4. An exception to this rule may be found at Hammath-Gader, which has a third row of columns as in the basilica-plans. See E.L. Sukenik, "The Ancient Synagogue of El-Hammeh," *Journal of the Palestine Oriental Society*, Volume XV, pp. 101-181 (1935), p. 122.

5. The references are collected in E.R. Goodenough, *Jewish Symbols In the Greco-Roman Period*, Volume I (New York, 1953), pp. 260-262. Most scholars believe the floor is a late one, to a time when human and animal representation had been restricted.

6. Decree of 415 C.E., Code of Theodosius II, Novels of Theodosius 3:3 (*The Theodosian Code*, Clyde Pharr (trans.) (Princeton, 1952), p. 489).

7. J.W. Crowfoot, *Early Churches In Palestine* (London, 1941), p. 125.

8. Belle D. Mazur dates this synagogue to the 4th century on the basis of the form of the Greek letters. Belle D. Mazur, *Studies On Jewry In Greece*, Volume I (Athens, 1935), pp. 27-28. Avi-Yonah dates the Aegina mosaic to the 6th century. It is interesting to compare the Aegina mosaic to the 4th century geometric mosaic at the synagogue of Apamaea, Syria, of which E.R. Goodenough remarks, "The mosaic itself is interesting as coming from a Greek-speaking community, at the period when the symbolic ornamentation of synagogues and graves was at its height, and yet not even a menorah is here." E.R. Goodenough, *Jewish Symbols In the Greco-Roman Period*, Volume II (New York, 1953), p. 84.

9. *Menahoth* 28b; *Abodah Zarah* 43a; *Rosh Hashanah* 24a, 24b. See "Candlestick," *Jewish Encyclopedia*, Volume III, pp. 531-533 (New York, 1902), p. 533.

10. I. Sonne, "Synagogue," *The Interpreter's Dictionary of the Bible*, Volume IV, pp. 476-491 (New York, 1962), pp. 487-488.

11. Gideon Foerster has recently suggested that the prohibition was limited to *metal* three dimensional representations of the Temple *menorah*. G. Foerster, "Some Menorah Reliefs From Galilee," *Israel Exploration Journal*, Volume XXIV, Nos. 3-4, pp. 191-196 (1974), p. 195, note 27. Another possible limitation on the prohibition may have been geographical. The prohibition appears in the Babylonian Talmud but not in the Palestinian Talmud. See J. Gutmann, "Prologomenon," *The Synagogue: Studies In Origins, Archaeology and Architecture*. J. Gutmann (ed.) (New York, 1975), p. xix.

12. E.R. Goodenough, *Jewish Symbols In the Greco-Roman Period*, Volume IV (New York, 1954), p. 71.

13. See, e.g., "Menorah," *Encyclopedia Judaica*, Volume XI (Jerusalem, 1971), pp. 1355-1370; W. Wirgin, "On the Shape of the Foot of the Menorah," *Israel Exploration Journal*, Volume XI, No. 3, pp. 151-154 (1961), p. 151.

14. Compare the rabbis' attempts from time to time to drop the Kol Nidre prayer from the Yom Kippur service. Herman Kreval, "The Curious Case of Kol Nidre," *Commentary*, Volume XXXVI, No. 4 (October, 1968), pp. 53-58.

15. See E.L. Sukenik, "The Ancient Synagogue of El-Hammeh," *Journal of the Palestine Oriental Society*, Volume XV, pp. 101-181 (1935), pp. 136-137.

16. A donation of two denarii is mentioned in an inscription at the synagogue of Ma'on. S. Levy *et. al.*, "The Ancient Synagogue of Ma'on (Nirim)," *Louis M. Rabinowitz Fund for the Exploration of Ancient Synagogues, Bulletin III*, pp. 6-40 (1960), p. 36. An inscription from the Aegina synagogue indicates that the cost of the synagogue was covered by revenues of 85 pieces of gold and offerings unto God of 105 pieces of gold. Belle D. Mazur, *Studies On Jewry In Greece*, Volume I (Athens, 1935), p. 28.

17. It has been suggested that the gold denari weighed about 5.45 grams in the 4th century C.E. S. Levy *et. al.*, "The Ancient Synagogue of Ma'on (Nirim)," *Louis M. Rabinowitz Fund for the Exploration of Ancient Synagogues, Bulletin III*, pp. 6-40 (Jerusalem, 1960), p. 40, note 29.

18. G. Foerster, "Some Menorah Reliefs from Galilee," *Israel Exploration Journal*, Vol. XXIV, Nos. 3-4, pp. 190-196 (1974), p. 196.

19. Z. Yeivin, "Inscribed Marble Fragments from the Khirbet Susiya Synagogue," *Israel Exploration Journal*, Vol. XXIV, Nos. 3-4, pp. 201-209 (1974), p. 207.

20. *Ibid.*

21. E.R. Goodenough, *Jewish Symbols In the Greco-Roman Period*, Volume I (New York, 1953), p. 267; Volume II, p. 79.

22. *Id.*, Vol. II, p. 79.

23. See S. Levy *et. al.*, "The Ancient Synagogue of Ma'on (Nirim)," *Louis M. Rabinowitz Fund for the Exploration of Ancient Synagogues, Bulletin III*, pp. 6-40 (1960), p. 27.

24. A.D. Trendall, *The Shellal Mosaic* (Canberra, 1942).

25. Actually Abraham only touches Isaac, but this is apparently this rude artist's attempt at portraying Isaac being held.

26. See J.W. Crowfoot, *Early Churches In Palestine* (London, 1941), p. 118.

27. E.L. Sukenik, *The Ancient Synagogue of Beth Alpha* (Jerusalem, 1932), p. 35.

Chapter 9
Out in the Field

1. See also the recent swastikas found in the synagogue of Ma'oz Hayyim. V. Tzaferis, Notes and News, *Israel Exploration Journal*, Vol. XXIV, No. 2, pp. 143-144 (1974).

2. This is not the only ancient synagogue which does not fit our typology. Other possibilities are Beth Shearim and Beth Shean.

Chapter 10
The Image in the Synagogue

1. Solomon J. Solomon, "Art and Judaism," *Jewish Quarterly Review*, Volume XIII, pp. 553-556 (New York, 1901), p. 553.

2. Ibid.

3. Bernard Berenson, *Aesthetics and History* (New York, 1948), p. 164 (New York, 1954), p. 180.

4. Exodus 20:4-5; Deuteronomy 5:8-9.

5. E.g., Deuteronomy 4:15-16; Deuteronomy 27:15; Leviticus 26:1.

6. Sigmund Freud, *Moses and Monotheism* (New York, 1955 (1935)), p. 144.

7. "Art Among the Ancient Hebrews," *Jewish Encyclopedia*, Volume II, pp. 138-141 (New York, 1902), p. 141. Alfred Werner, the Jewish art critic, wrote of his own youth in Vienna: "I remember how the anti-semitic literature emphasized an alleged 'color-blindness' of the Jewish race and how some of the teachers at my *gymnasium* openly declared that Jews were biologically less capable of expressing themselves in color and line than in words." Alfred Werner, "What Is Jewish Art?" *Judaism*, Volume XI, No. 1, pp. 32-43 (Winter, 1962), p. 33.

8. Hans Kohn, *Prophets and People* (New York, 1946).

9. Herbert Howarth, "Jewish Art and the Fear of the Image," *Commentary*, Volume IX, pp. 142-150 (February, 1950), p. 142.

10. Ibid.

11. D. Kaufman, "Art In the Synagogue," *Jewish Quarterly Review*, Volume IX, pp. 254-262 (New York, 1897), pp. 254-255.

12. Solomon J. Solomon, "Art and Judaism," *Jewish Quarterly Review*, Volume XIII, pp. 553-566 (New York, 1901), p. 554.

13. *Abodah Zarah 50a; Pesahim 104a; P.T. Megillah 3:2.*

14. Exodus 37; II Chronicles 3-4; as to images in Solomon's palace, see II Chronicles 9.

15. I Kings 6-7.

16. Exekiel 41:18-20.

17. Joseph Gutmann, "The 'Second Commandment' and the Image of Judaism," *Hebrew Union College Annual*, Volume XXXII (Cincinnati, 1961), pp. 161-174.

18. Josephus, *The Wars of the Jews*, Book I 33:2 and Book II 9:2. Whether for the sake of consistency, as Rabbi Gutmann suggests, or simply because Josephus himself otherwise interpreted the Second Commandment very strictly, Josephus even condemns Solomon for putting images in the Temple and in his palace. Josephus, *The Antiquities of the Jews*, Book VIII 7:5.

19. However, there is a question about whether the base of the *menorah* is genuine. See E.L. Sukenik, *Ancient Synagogues In Palestine and Greece*, (London, 1934), p. 63; "Menorah," *Encyclopedia Judaica*, Volume XI, pp. 1355-1371 (Jerusalem, 1971), pp. 1364-1366.

20. *Abodah Zarah 40b.*

21. E.L. Sukenik, *Ancient Synagogues In Palestine and Greece* (London, 1934), pp. 27-28; J.N. Epstein, "Additional Fragments of the Jerushalmi," *Tarbiz*, Volume III, No. 1. pp. 15-26 (Jerusalem, 1931), p. 15 (Hebrew). *P.T. Abodah Zarah, 41d I. 37-42 a I .7.*

22. E.L. Sukenik, *Ancient Synagogues In Palestine and Greece* (London, 1934), p. 28. *Cf.* Rachel Wischnitzer, "Jewish Pictorial Art In the Late Classical Period," *Jewish Art*, C. Roth (ed.), pp. 83-92 (Connecticut, 1971), p. 88, who says that the reference may be to *Abun* II.

23. E.L. Sukenik, *Ancient Synagogues In Palestine and Greece* (London, 1934), p. 28.

24. E.E. Urbach, "The Rabbinical Laws of Idolatry In the Second and Third Centuries In the Light of Archaeological and Historical Facts," *Israel Exploration Journal*, Volume IX, No. 3 (Jerusalem, 1959), pp. 149-165; *Israel Exploration Journal*, Volume IX, No. 4 (Jerusalem, 1959), pp. 229-245.

25. Id. at p. 236.

26. Joseph Gutmann, "Prologomenon," *No Graven Image*, J. Gutmann (ed.), pp. XI-LXIII (New York, 1971), p. XV.

27. Saul Lieberman, *Hellenism In Jewish Palestine* (New York, 1950), pp. 120-121.

28. However, the *Tosephta* itself tells us that, in Jerusalem before the destruction, there were faces of all creatures except men. *Tosephta Abodah Zarah* 5(6):2, and the Patriarch Gamaliel used a seal with faces on it. See E.L. Sukenik, *Ancient Synagogues In Palestine and Greece* (London, 1934), p. 64.

29. F.M. Biebel, "Mosaics," *Gerasa, City of the Decapolis*, C.H. Kraeling (ed.), pp. 297-352 (New Haven, 1938), p. 324; G.M.A. Hanfmann, "The Ancient Synagogue of Sardis," *Fourth World Congress of Jewish Studies, Papers I*, pp. 37-42 (Jerusalem, 1967), p. 41.

30. "Art," *Encyclopedia Judaica*, Volume III, pp. 499-644 (Jerusalem, 1971), p. 521; Cecil Roth, "Introduction," *Jewish Art*, C. Roth (ed.) (Connecticut, 1971), p. 14; E.L. Sukenik, *Ancient Synagogues In Palestine and Greece* (London, 1934), p. 65; Cf. M. Avi-Yonah, *Oriental Art In Roman Palestine* (Rome, 1961), p. 42, who sees the Jewish aniconic attitude as a protest against and in opposition to the use of images by the church. But *cf.* M. Avi-Yonah, "Jewish Art," *The Encyclopedia of World Art*, Volume VIII, pp. 898-920 (London, 1963), pp. 900, 909, 914, 915.

Chapter 11
Pagan Symbols in Synagogue Art

1. H. Kohl and C. Watzinger, *Antike Synagogen In Galilaea* (Leipzig, 1916).

2. This theory was first proposed by H. H. Kitchener, "Synagogues of Galilee," *Palestine Exploration Quarterly*, pp. 123-129 (July, 1878), p. 128

3. By contrast, the gift of a single golden *menorah* by the Emperor Antoninus (Caracalla) is mentioned in the Talmud.

4. E.E. Urbach, "The Rabbinical Laws of Idolatry In the Second and Third Centuries In the Light of Archaeological and Historical Facts," *Israel Exploration Journal*, Volume IX, No. 3, pp. 149-165 (Jerusalem, 1959), p. 149.

5. E.R. Goodenough, *Jewish Symbols In the Greco-Roman Period*, Volumes I-XIII, (New York, 1953-1968).

6. E.R. Goodenough, *Jewish Symbols In the Greco-Roman Period*, Volume I (New York, 1953), p. 58.

7. In Volume XII, containing his summary and conclusions, he reacted strongly to this kind of praise: "Scholars have repeatedly said to me 'At least you will always be remembered and used for your collection of material . . .' I have not spent thirty years as a mere collector: I was trying to make a point." E.R. Goodenough, *Jewish Symbols In the Greco-Roman Period*, Volume XII (New York, 1965), preface.

8. E.R. Goodenough, *Jewish Symbols In the Greco-Roman Period*, Volume IV (New York, 1954), p. 211. According to Goodenough, "Mysticism is the attempt here and now to partake of the eternal Reality which normally we expect fully to share only after death." E.R. Goodenough, *Jewish Symbols In the Greco-Roman Period*, Volume I (New York, 1953), p. 266.

9. Morton Smith, "Goodenough's *Jewish Symbols* In Retrospect," *The Synagogue: Studies In Origins, Archaeology and Architecture*, J. Gutmann (ed.), pp. 194-209 (New York, 1975), p. 195 (Reprinted from *Journal of Biblical Literature*, Volume LXXXVI, pp. 53-68 (1967), p. 54).

10. T.H. Gaster, "Pagan Ideas and the Jewish Mind," *Commentary*, Volume XVII, No. 2 (February, 1954), pp. 185-190.

11. Morton Smith, "Goodenough's *Jewish Symbols* In Retrospect," *The Synagogue: Studies In Origins, Archaeology and Architecture*, J. Gutmann (ed.), pp. 194-209 (New York, 1975), p. 200 (Reprinted from *Journal of Biblical Literature*, Volume LXXXVI, pp. 53-68 (1967), p. 59).

12. N. Avigad, "The Beth She'arim Necropolis," *Antiquity and Survival*, Volume II, Nos. 2-3, pp. 244-261 (Hague and Jerusalem, 1957), p. 258.

13. The sarcophagus may have been in re-use at Beth Shearim—which is different from an intrusion—but this does not alter the nature of the problem with which we are concerned. See M. Avi-Yonah, "The Leda Sarcophagus From Beth She'arim," *Scripta Hierosolymitana*, Moshe Barasch (ed.), Volume XXIV, pp. 9-21 (Jerusalem, 1972), pp. 19, 21.

14. N. Avigad, "The Beth She'arim Necropolis," *Antiquity and Survival*, Volume II, Nos. 2-3, pp. 244-261 (Hague and Jerusalem, 1957), p. 258.

15. Ibid.

16. M. Avi-Yonah, "Goodenough's Evaluation of the Dura Paintings: A Critique," *The Dura Europos Synagogue: A Re-evaluation*, J. Gutmann (ed.), pp. 117-135 (Montana, 1973), p. 132.

17. Ibid.

18. Morton Smith, "Goodenough's *Jewish Symbols* In Retrospect," *The Synagogue: Studies In Origins, Archaeology*

and Architecture, J. Gutmann (ed.), pp. 194-209 (New York, 1975), p. 206 (Reprinted from *Journal of Biblical Literature*, Volume LXXXVI, pp. 53-68 (1967), p. 65).

19. N. Avigad, "The Beth She'arim Necropolis," *Antiquity and Survival*, Volume II, Nos. 2-3, pp. 244-261 (Hague and Jerusalem, 1957), p. 258. See also, Rachel Wischnitzer, "Jewish Pictorial Art In the Late Classical Period," *Jewish Art*, C. Roth (ed.), pp. 83-92 (Connecticut, 1971), p. 90, who suggests that perhaps Helios was simply a conventional calendar figure. The lengths to which scholars will go to give a satisfactory "Jewish" explanation of this apparently embarrassing pagan symbol may be seen in Wischnitzer's further suggestion that the Helios in his chariot may have been transmogrified in Jewish minds to the prophet Elijah ascending to heaven in his fiery chariot.

20. Morton Smith, "Goodenough's *Jewish Symbols* In Retrospect," *The Synagogue: Studies In Origins, Archaeology and Architecture*, J. Gutmann (ed.), pp. 194-209 (New York, 1975), p. 207 (Reprinted from *Journal of Biblical Literature*, Volume LXXXVI, pp. 53-68 (1967), p. 66).

21. *Cf.* M. Avi-Yonah's equally vague statement that "it is clear that these symbols were used in a general and non-pagan sense." Synagogue-Architecture, *Encyclopedia Judaica*, Volume XV, pp. 595-600 (Jerusalem, 1971), p. 597.

22. H.L. Gordon, "The Basilica and the Stoa In Early Rabbinical Literature," *The Art Bulletin*, Volume XIII, No. 3, pp. 353-375 (Chicago, 1931), pp. 355.

23. Elias J. Bickerman, "Symbolism In the Dura Synagogue," *Harvard Theological Review*, Volume LVIII, No. 1, pp. 127-151 (Cambridge, 1965), p. 130. As Saul Lieberman has pointed out in *Greek In Jewish Palestine* (New York, 1942), p. 30, the Palestinian Talmud records that some Palestinian Jews even recited the *Shema* in Greek. See also, Saul Lieberman, *Hellenism In Jewish Palestine* (New York, 1950).

24. To be fair to Goodenough, it may be that he himself retreated somewhat in later years from the extreme position taken in his earlier volumes regarding the existence of the "other" Judaism, and concentrated instead on the source of the pagan influence, which, as he rightly observed, lay outside the rabbinic tradition. Consider the following quotation from a 1961 article: "We need not dispute whether the Jews at Dura, Randanini, Hamman Lif, Beth Alpha, and Capernaum were either 'totally different' from the rabbis, or thought identically with them. Either extreme seems absurd to me. The question is whether, as we look for the incentive which demanded and produced the art, we may find it in the rabbinic tradition." E.R. Goodenough, "The Rabbis and Jewish Art in the Greco-Roman Period," *Hebrew Union College Annual*, Volume XXXII, pp. 269-279 (Cincinnati, 1961), p. 278.

25. T.H. Gaster, "Pagan Ideas and the Jewish Mind," *Commentary*, Volume XVII, No. 2, pp. 185-190 (February, 1954), p. 190.

26. A. Reifenberg, *Ancient Hebrew Arts* (New York, 1950), p. 114. See also, *Sefer Yetzirah* (Book of Creation).

27. Dr. Lee Levine has called my attention to the fact that a Jewish prayer to Helios is recorded in *Sefer Ha-Razim*, M. Margalioth (ed.) (Jerusalem, 1966).

28. M. Avi-Yonah, "Ancient Synagogues," *Ariel*, No. 32, pp. 29-43 (Jerusalem, 1973), p. 43. However, Avi-Yonah's statement that the zodiac and Helios "were divested of all idolatrous associations" seems extreme. For an interesting, and possibly correct, theory on how the zodiac secretly depicted Judaism's triumph over Rome, see Isaiah Sonne, "The Zodiac Theme In Ancient Synagogues and In Hebrew Printed Books," *Studies In Bibliography and Booklore*, Volume I, No. 1 (June, 1953), pp. 3-13. According to Sonne, in Jewish zodiacs, Cancer, the secret sign of Israel, was placed on top, over Helios in his chariot; and Leo, the sign of Rome, was shown in decline. Sonne's interpretations of the zodiac is rejected in Rachel Wischnitzer, "The Beth Alpha Mosaic," *Jewish Social Studies*, Volume XVII, No. 2, pp. 133-144 (New York, 1955), p. 143.

29. Morton Smith, "Goodenough's *Jewish Symbols* In Retrospect," *The Synagogue: Studies In Origins, Archaeology and Architecture*, J. Gutmann (ed.), pp. 194-209 (New York, 1975), p. 202 (Reprinted from *Journal of Biblical Literature*, Volume LXXXVI, pp. 53-68 (1967), p. 61).

Chapter 12
Recent Discoveries at Ostia and Sardis

1. See Harry J. Leon, *The Jews of Ancient Rome* (Philadelphia, 1960), pp. 135-166.

2. See Maria F. Squarciapino, "The Synagogue at Ostia," *Archaeology*, Volume XVI, No. 3, pp. 194-203 (September, 1963), p. 203.

3. Y. Shiloh, "Torah Scrolls and the Menorah Plaque From Sardis," *Israel Exploration Journal*, Volume XVIII, pp. 54-57 (1968), p. 55.

4. G.M.A. Hanfmann *et. al.*, "The Ninth Campaign at Sardis (1966)," *Bulletin of the American Schools of Oriental Research*, No. 187, pp. 9-62 (October, 1967), p. 50.

5. G.M.A. Hanfmann *et. al.*, "The Sixth Campaign at Sardis (1963)," *Bulletin of the American Schools of Oriental Research*, No. 174, pp. 3-58 (April, 1964), p. 38.

6. G.M.A. Hanfmann, "The Ancient Synagogue of Sardis," *Fourth World Congress of Jewish Studies, Papers I*, pp. 37-42 (Jerusalem, 1967), p. 40.

7. In the description of architectural features of the Sardis synagogue, I have in general followed Andrew R. Seager, "The Building History of the Sardis Synagogue," *American Journal of Archaeology*, Volume CXXVI, No. 4 (October, 1972), pp. 425-435. In addition to the articles cited in previous footnotes herein and the preliminary reports cited in Seager's article, I have also found helpful, David G. Mitten, "A New Look at Ancient Sardis," *The Biblical Archaeologist*, Volume XXIX, No. 2 (May, 1966), pp. 38-68.

LIST OF ILLUSTRATIONS

ILLUSTRATION CREDITS

F. Alinari, 54, 56, 147; Archeological Exploration of Sardis, 169 (top), 170, 172 (both), 173, Samuele Bacchiocchi, 164-165; Dan Bahat, 14; Ban Barag, 132, 133, 134 (both), 135, 136, 139 (both), 140, 141; Meir Ben-Dov, 38, 39; Meron Benvenisti, 34; Werner Braun, 16, 27, 127; Werner Braun, Yael Baun Archives, 25, 31, 32, 153, 154, 159 (bottom); Ecole Francaise d'Archeologie, Athens, 44 (both); David Harris, 59, 60; The Hebrew University of Jerusalem, 111 (left); Milton Heiberg, 100; Israel Department of Antiquities, 11, 19, 47, 49, 109, 110, 117, 129; Israel Exploration Journal, 13, 119; Israel Museum, 144, 145; Eric M. Meyers, 100, 101, 104; Garo Nablandian, 62, 114; Asher Ovadiah, 111 (bottom); Princeton University Press (Copyright 1964 Bollingen Foundation), 90 (top); Zev Radovan, 28, 40, 47, 65, 66, 67, 68, 71, 73, 74, 98 (both), 111 (top), 118, 128, 130, 149, 155, 157; Hershel Shanks, 61 (both), 75, 76 (top); Suzanne Singer, 76 (bottom left and bottom right); Soprintendenza Alle Antichita' Di Ostia, 167 (both); Maria Floriani Squarciapino, 166; Yigael Yadin, 18, 22, 24, 26, 159 (top); Yale University (Copyright 1964 by Bollingen Foundation), 95; Zev Yeivin, 102, 103.

INDEX

189